PANDORA PRESS

THE DORA RUSSELL READER

THE DORA RUSSELL READER

57 years of writing and journalism, 1925-1982

Foreword by Dale Spender

P A N D O R A   P R E S S

Routledge & Kegan Paul
London, Melbourne and Henley

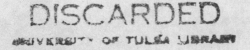

First published in 1983
by Pandora Press
(Routledge & Kegan Paul plc)
39 Store Street, London WC1E 7DD, England,
464 St Kilda Road, Melbourne,
Victoria 3004, Australia, and
Broadway House, Newtown Road,
Henley-on-Thames, Oxon RG9 1EN, England
Photoset in 10 on 11½ Century Schoolbook by
Kelly Typesetting Ltd, Bradford-on-Avon, Wiltshire
and printed in Great Britain by
Cox & Wyman Ltd

British Library Cataloguing in Publication Data

Russell, Dora

The Dora Russell reader: 57 years of writing and
journalism, 1925–1982.
1. General 2. Politics 3. History 4. Feminism
I. Title
305.4'2   HQ1154

ISBN 0–86358–020–3

CONTENTS

FOREWORD

Sexual politics—racism, militarism, industrialism—these are some of the issues of modern times and issues about which Dora Russell has much to say. It is not perhaps surprising that she should be so passionately concerned with these problems – but what *is* undeniably surprising is that they should be problems which have been her central focus for more than sixty years. Some of us may have believed that these contemporary issues were 'new' issues, but the record of Dora Russell's understandings and insights reveals that they are very old issues. Her own writing across the decades since the early 1920s helps to suggest that the analysis she provided – and the possible solutions she put forward – are just as relevant and realistic today as they were when she first proposed them.

Through some of the writings of Dora Russell over the last sixty years we are provided with a view of a changing world, which in itself is valuable, and which helps and enhances our present understandings. But this is not all we are offered: we can also witness the continuity of one woman's commitment and insights, and this is a rare privilege in a male-dominated society in which too frequently a woman's voice is interrupted and silenced. If we can locate them, it is possible to find many women whose reflections on a decade, or a generation, may allow us a glimpse of a particular period through women's eyes, but few are the accounts of women which span decades and which help to reveal both the transitory and the constant problems that have been faced. From some of the writings of Dora Russell we can begin to appreciate that in the twentieth century – a century customarily characterised by its accelerated rate of change and progress—there is much that has not been modified at all. As far as she is concerned the world view of our society – which she suggests is the origin of many of our present problems – has changed little.

Basically her thesis is very simple, and it is one which was 'revived' again by feminists in the 1970s, although they were not to know that Dora Russell had said it all before – again and again. The world view which is society's view, Dora Russell argues, is solely a *man's* view, and because much of human experience and understanding is omitted from it, it is both a source of the problem and an obstacle to solutions.

According to Dora Russell, this is no accident. Men, she says, have prided themselves on their *intellect* and have deliberately attempted to eliminate from their frame of reference that which they have called *subjective*, that which they term emotion and feeling and which they see as a source of contamination. Yet the subjective, emotion and feeling, are as necessarily human as the intellect, and it is precisely emotion and feeling which are required if we are to overcome some of our present problems.

But emotion and feeling have been associated with women, and this gives rise to another problem. Women are not valued, and if the subjective is to play an equal part in forming society's view of the world, then either the association between women and the subjective will have to be broken – or women and their qualities will have to be valued equally with men. To Dora Russell's mind, men showed little inclination to accommodate women as equals in the 1920s and they show little inclination to do so today. Part of the fabric of the male view of the world, she argues persuasively, is the desire to control. This is why men seek to dominate; it is why they have developed their intellect at the expense of their emotions in their bid to control nature and women. It is why men have turned to machines to solve human problems, she asserts.

This thesis of Dora Russell's, which has remained constant over sixty years (often in the face of hostility), has led her to outline and analyse many social issues. Sexual politics – or 'sex antagonism' – is a foundation stone in her understandings, and from it she has built her theory that only men could have invented the machines which now rule our lives, from it she has forged her explanations about the absence of *feeling* in our arrangements for society, in our consideration of the next generation.

Morality is a keystone in Dora Russell's view of the world: she does not hesitate to claim that there is right and wrong. She has never faltered in her stand of declaring certain practices wrong – no matter how fashionable they may be or how unpopular her criticisms may prove – and she has never wavered in her commitment to do what she believes is right. This is one of the reasons why her philosophy has stood the test of time – even though it may be unfashionable and unpopular today to insist on a *moral* view and to suggest that it is *feeling* that the modern world needs.

For me it has been a privilege and a joy to know Dora Russell. Although she has endured much in her life, her optimism and her faith in her fellow human beings (an 'emotional' rather than a 'rational' stand) are a source of inspiration for many of us today. From her way of understanding and living we can learn much, and perhaps we can build on the tradition that she has helped to generate.

Dale Spender
London, 1983

Part One

HYPATIA
OR WOMAN AND KNOWLEDGE
1925

In the long struggle for full human rights, women have often raised
the issue of sexuality. Dora Russell was reared in an era when
discussions of sexuality were virtually taboo, and she was a young
woman at a time when many feminists were asserting their right to
'live like men', when they were demanding not just the opportunity
to vote but the opportunity to leave behind the private and
protected sphere of the home and to become independent wage
earners. By raising issues about women's sexuality, about the right
to a satisfactory sex life and safe and readily available forms of
birth control, Dora Russell did little to endear herself to many of the
pious and proper people of her time and she was snidely (and
erroneously) regarded as permissive: but by cautioning many of
her contemporaries against the dangers of 'living like men', and by
demanding the right to motherhood, she antagonised some
women who thought such a stance reactionary. Never one to think
that the best course was necessarily the most popular course, Dora
Russell continued to argue for women's right to motherhood and to
wage earning, in a way that was mutually enhancing. She has
always believed that it would not be difficult to organise society so
that all members could work and play, to make and to nurture, in a
productive way. That it has been made difficult – even impossible –
for women to combine work and mothering in a constructive
manner is for Dora Russell part of the evidence that it has been men
who have been responsible for our social arrangements. *Hypatia* is
reprinted here in its entirety.

PREFACE

Hypatia was a University lecturer denounced by Church dignitaries and torn to pieces by Christians. Such will probably be the fate of this book: therefore it bears her name. What I have written here I believe, and shall not retract or change for similar episcopal denunciation.

Dora Russell
January, 1925.

Chapter I

JASON AND MEDEA

Is there a Sex War?

A feature of modern life is that matrimonial quarrels, like modern war, are carried on on a large scale, involving not individuals, nor even small groups of individuals, but both sexes and whole classes of society. In the past, Jason and Medea, neither of them quite an exemplary character, measured their strength against one another as individuals; and, though each voiced the wrongs and the naked brutality of their sex, it did not occur to either to seek in politics or in social reform a solution or a compromise. Jason, indeed, as the reactionary face to face with a turbulent and insurgent female, called to his aid the powers of kingship and the State – to suppress and exile, but not to remedy. Medea, driven mad – like so many able and remarkable women – by the contempt and ingratitude of men as individuals or in the mass, and aware that the law was a mockery where she was concerned, expressed herself in savage protest after the manner of a militant suffragette. While I can open my newspaper to-day and read of mothers desperate with hunger, misery, or rage drowning themselves and their children, I cannot bring myself to look upon Medea as some elemental being from a dark and outrageous past. As for Jason, he never did appear to anybody as other than an ordinary male.

During the last twenty or twenty-five years, when women were struggling for their right as citizens to a vote and to a decent education, began what has been called the sex war. No woman would deny that we began it, in the sense that we were rebels against a system of masculine repression which had lasted almost unbroken since the beginning of history. In a similar sense, the proletarian to-day begins the class war. Those who remember the heroic battles of suffrage days know

3

that the sequence of events was as follows: We made our just demands and were met with ridicule. We followed with abuse – all the pent-up anger, misery, and despair of centuries of thwarted instinct and intelligence. Man retaliated with rotten eggs. We replied with smashed windows; he with prison and torture. People forget so readily, that it is well to remember that this was in the immediate past; it is not a nightmare picture of one of those future sex wars with which our modern Jasons delight to terrify the timorous of both sexes.

Is there a sex war? There has been. It was a disgraceful exhibition, and would not have come to a truce so soon, but that it was eclipsed by the still more disgraceful exhibition of the European War. In 1918 they bestowed the vote, just as they dropped about a few Dames and M.B.E.s, as a reward for our services in helping the destruction of our offspring. Had we done it after the fashion of Medea, the logical male would have been angry. They gave the vote to the older women, who were deemed less rebellious. Such is the discipline of patriotism and marriage, as it is understood by most women, that the mother will sacrifice her son with more resigned devotion than the younger woman brings to the loss of her lover. There may be more in this than discipline. If honesty of thought, speech, and action were made possible for women, it might transpire that on the average a woman's love for her mate is more compelling than love for her offspring. Maternal instinct – genuine, not simulated – is rarer, but, when found, more enduring.

There was a promise, as yet unredeemed by any political party – for the politician has yet to be found who will realize that the sex problem is as fundamental in politics as the class war, and more fundamental than foreign trade and imperial expansion – to extend this franchise on equal terms with men. 'Good fellowship' between the sexes as between the classes was the key-note of the war. It was held that women had proved their mettle and that mutual aid was to be the basis of all future activities, public and private. The sex question was deemed settled, and everyone was led to suppose that all inequalities would be gradually eliminated. On this partial victory and this promise feminists called a truce, and abandoned the tactics of militarism.

But you never know where you have Jason. He was a soldier, mark you, and a gentleman. Forbidden open warfare, he takes to sniping. He snipes the married women out of those posts for which they are peculiarly fitted – as teachers or maternity doctors – although it is against the law to bar women from any public activity on the ground of marriage. He cheats unemployed women out of their unemployment insurance more craftily and brutally than he cheats his fellow-men. Instead of realizing that the competition of women in industry and the professions is a competition of population pressure rather than of sex, he seeks by every means in his power to drive woman back to matrimonial dependence and an existence on less than half a miserably inadequate income; and then he mocks at her when she claims the right to stem the inevitable torrent of children whose advent will but aggravate man's difficulties as well as her own. But worse than all the sniping is the smoke-screen of propaganda. While feminists have, in a large measure, stayed their hand, anybody who has anything abusive to say of women, whether ancient or modern, can command a vast public in the popular press and a ready agreement from the average publisher.

It is a very insidious propaganda. Thus the fashion-papers tell us that grandmamma's ways are coming back into their own; elsewhere we are flattered for the frank honesty of the modern girl and then warned not to ask for equal pay or opportunity.[1] Again, we hear that woman, like the Labour Party when in office, has done nothing with the opportunities given her by the vote; or that the country rejected the women candidates wholesale. This, regardless of the fact that the steady increase of the Labour poll has been due in great part to the votes and more to the organization and propaganda of large numbers of intelligent working women who know not only what they want, but how to get it. They are backed now by many of the middle-class women who were young enough to be revolted by war politics in 1914, and are old enough to claim their citizenship in 1924. Hundreds of thousands of others, now between twenty and thirty, mothers, professional and working women, will make themselves heard before long. To them, the principle of feminine equality is as natural as drawing breath – they are neither oppressed by tradition nor worn by rebellion. I venture to think that, had the Labour Party machine been less dominated by the masculine perspective, to which the equal franchise Bill was a matter of secondary importance, they would not have lost so heavily in the 1924 election. Votes for women at 21 would have greatly increased the poll of many Labour candidates. I have seen young mothers almost sobbing outside the polling-station on polling-day because they had no vote to cast for the future of themselves and their children. As for the defeat of women candidates, everybody, including the leader-writers who spread the adverse propaganda, knew perfectly well that the majority of them stood in constituencies where even a man of their party would not have had the ghost of a chance. Here again Jason at headquarters displayed his well-known chivalry.

It is no part of my thesis to maintain that women display their feminism in proportion as they vote for any particular political party – Labour, for example. But I do suggest that it is the progressive working woman rather than the woman of the middle class who will in the future make the most important contribution to the thought of feminism and to a solution of our practical difficulties. One of the most inveterate anti-feminists, the author of *Lysistrata*,* as an avowed anti-democrat, has based his thesis and his strictures on observations that do not go beyond the bounds of upper- and middle-class people, barely even beyond the bounds of the night club or the suburban dance-hall. In his eyes we are to blame for everything. Our worst crime is to 'blaspheme life and man'; our next, not to have prevented food being put into tins; our next, to have adhered faithfully to that ascetic view of life and sex so firmly instilled into us by medieval monks and bullying Puritan fathers and brothers. We are to blame for the industrial revolution in that we let weaving, spinning, milling, and baking go out of our hands. We are to blame for

* *Lysistrata, or Woman's Future and Future Woman* by Anthony M. Ludovici was an anti-feminist book published, like *Hypatia*, in the To-day and To-morrow series by Kegan Paul, Trench, Trubner.

the iniquities of doctors in that we did not maintain our position as the dispensers of healing potions and simples. We are to blame in that we have not learned to bring forth our children without pain, those children whose brows bear the marks of obstetric instruments that were used to spare their mothers, and whose lips have not been laid to those inhuman mothers' breasts. (There are no scars of war, O Jason!) Where is salvation for us, and how shall we rid us of the burden of our iniquity? We who have aspired to let science build our children outside their mothers' bodies must humble ourselves once more and take upon us the whole duty of woman. We must use our votes to restore aristocracy[2] and take the food out of tins; spin and weave, no doubt, the while we nurse and bear our yearly child, delivering it over to infanticide when necessary, since birth-control is artificial and displeasing to the male. In our leisure moments – of which, doubtless, we shall find many under this humane *régime* – we are to discover by what means of diet, or exercise it may be, we can fulfil our maternal functions with pleasure instead of suffering.

A joke you say? No, no, my poor Medea, it is a man called Rousseau, risen from the dead. Not long ago he preached this sort of thing to women who pinched their waists and wore a dozen petticoats. They were not educated enough to follow Voltaire, so they listened to what Rousseau called the Voice of Nature. Soon thereafter, they found they were being abused for being less civilized, more ape-like than the male, irrational and unsuited to take a part in public life. So they tried again, poor things, and then there was an awful thing called the Industrial Revolution, and the food got into tins. They may be pardoned, as may all of us, if at this point they became a little bewildered. Some people blamed science, some civilization, some the meat-trusts and the millers, but the true culprit, as ever, was Woman. A thousand voices cried her down – she hadn't enough children; she had too many; she was an ape; she was a dressed-up doll; she was a Puritan; she was an immoral minx; she was uneducated; they had taught her too much. Her pinched waist was formerly abused – now it was her slim and boyish body. Eminent surgeons[3] committed themselves to the view that the boyish figure with its pliable rubber bust-bodices and corselets would be the ruin of the race, that race which had been superbly undegenerate through four centuries of armour-plate corset and eighteen-inch waists, that race which, then or now, can hardly compete in toughness with the Chinese, among whom the boyish figure has been for centuries the ideal, and whose women cannot conceivably be accused of shirking any of the responsibilities of maternity. Others told us that the woman-doctor has no nerve to tend confinements, and conveniently forgot that, since the world began, and until quite modern times, it is women who have ministered to one another in that agony which now as in the past is the lot of every mother. Is there truth in the words of Jason? Is there truth or justice in the passion of Medea? Let us not ask the protagonists, but let us summon the inquiring intelligence of Hypatia to find us a way out of the intolerable tangle in which their quarrelling has landed us.

Chapter II

ARTEMIS

The Early Struggles of Feminism

When the feminist struggle began during the last century, ignorance and beauty were the two qualities most admired in women. It is necessary to remind our masculine critics what was the soil from which the feminist movement sprang and what the current morality which influenced its direction. It was customary in those days to make fun of old or ugly women and to scorn those who showed any signs of intelligence. A man chose a young, beautiful, and blushing creature for his bride, and transformed her by one year of marriage and one childbirth into a gentle and submissive matron. Ugly or intelligent women, for the most part, paid a heavy price. Not only were they rejected in youth, and starved of all their natural joys, but as 'old maids' they were the object of general scorn and derision. Small wonder that women adopted artificial hindrances to their native intelligence. Strongest of all the taboos laid by masculine custom and religion on feminine minds was that regarding sex-knowledge. Their purity was to be preserved only by ignorance, and even as matrons and mothers it was scarcely decent for them to refer to any of the physical changes of their bodies. It is impossible to over-estimate the strength of this tradition, or the harm which has been worked by it to the cause of women.

The feminists were, and are still, howled down by men on the pretence that they invented chastity and scorn of bodily values. History disproves such a ridiculous assertion. The early feminists were what history and tradition made them, and could not at the time of their rebellion have been otherwise. The origin of the stupid ideal of womanhood against which men as well as women to-day are still fighting was the asceticism of the Christian religion; and, unless St. Paul was a woman in disguise, I fail to see how woman is to be blamed for a conception of her place and duty from which she has suffered more than anybody else. Before the conversion of the West to Christianity, barbarian women of the North enjoyed a certain rough equality with their husbands. They stride through the sagas, these fierce women, brides of heroes, glad to reward the warrior with their favours, quick to avenge an insult or a wrong. They had no need to stoop to cajolery. Savage and untamed, they were the fit and equal mates of savage men.

Then came the monks, and the white wimples and courtly dresses and chivalry, chants and cathedrals, and meek and reverent casting up and casting down of eyes. The savage breast that had swelled and throbbed untrammelled in love or anger learnt to flutter and to sigh. Quenched were the fires of Brunhilde, her sunlit rock deserted. Agnes and Mary, tamed and pious, sat cooing in the shade. But for meekness and maternity, the early days of asceticism might have seen a crusade to destroy that temptress – woman. Barely allowed a soul, she slipped through a life of oblivion, praying that it might be a pretty crown with which Heaven would reward her patience and submission at the last. Then came the Puritans and denied her even that, substituting ugliness in this life as well as the negation of body, and a heaven of people in starched nightshirts, rendered oblivious to the horrid spectacle of their figures by the still more horrid chanting of their nasal psalms.

A breath of rationalism – brief, soon choked, a breath of 'nature' – and so to crinolines, pantalettes, and a life still lived in terror of hell-fire, terror of parents, dread of husband, horror of the least breath of adverse public opinion. Any one who reads the *Fairchild Family* must marvel that from such nerve-destroying parental tyranny and the intolerable weight of prejudice and religious superstition the nine-teenth-century woman ever found the courage to rebel.

Was it astonishing that the revolt had in it something frenzied and ascetic – that it seemed to express the anger of the spinster thwarted and despised in the current scheme of values? I do not think the pioneers were so much Puritan as votaries, hanging the tablet of each achievement in the temple of Athene or of Artemis, pressing on, breathless, swift of foot, sure of aim, in dread of the fate of Atalanta whom the Golden Apples lured to destruction and the marital embrace. 'Chaste as the icicle, that hangs on Dian's temple.' They had need to be, perhaps, who, in an atmosphere of swoons and ringlets, won for us schools and colleges, free limbs, health and the open air; unlocked for us the classics, science, medicine, the history of our world; drew us from our paltry, ladylike accomplishments; wrote upon our school-books: 'Knowledge is now no more a fountain sealed,' and flung wide the gate into the world.

They, these pioneers, childless, unwed, created and bore thousands of women, made them anew, body and soul, for lives of mental and physical activity unknown in the past to any but the very exceptional few. Just like the new learning of the Renaissance to men's minds in Europe was the opening of high school and university to the feminine mind of to-day. Thousands of women of the last generation and this, who would otherwise have passed their existence in genteel poverty and vacancy of mind, have found their happiness in teaching, in medicine, or in some other profession. Thousands of mothers have watched with delight the unfolding of their children's minds, and enjoyed co-operating over 'lessons' and arguing politics with the adolescent.

We, who in a sense are the children of the feminist pioneers, whose thoughts embrace the universe, whose lives are one long round of mental and physical delight, at times intense to ecstasy – we at least will pay our tribute to those who lit the sacred fires, before we take up pen and paper to criticize.

When one reads the lamentations of would-be intelligent men about the iniquities of modern young people, chiefly those of the female sex, one cannot but laugh at their method of approach. It would seem according to them that our modern women just happen like that: no one had a part in forming their bodies or in training their minds. In so far as these people consider education or early training at all, it is to blaspheme at the sex-hating feminists who have trained modern women to dispense with their birth-right – the love of man. How this squares with the wail of the Bishops against the sexual immorality of the younger generation we will leave Jason or the eloquent author of *Lysistrata* to decide. Our business is not to condemn woman, past or present, but to chronicle faithfully the forces that have made her, and the aspirations which will mould her future. For she, and she alone, shall be the arbiter of her fate, and neither man nor creed stand between her and the realization of her ideals. Men have blasphemed woman and life too long, and it will not be until the issues are clearer, the battle more advanced, that the basis for co-operation between man and woman can be finally established. There is too much evidence at present that man, professing friendship and concern, is still ready to snatch from us what little we have won.

To those elderly gentlemen, then, who watch with horror the upper- and middle-class woman perpetrating similar follies to those of upper- and middle-class men, the first question we would put is: 'What education did they give their daughters, and what was taught to their mothers before them? What were the current ideas about feminine destiny which encircled them in their impressionable years?' Many would answer, still far too many, that their daughters were given the education of a gentlewoman and fitted to become the wives of gentlemen. This we know of old. The lady eats, drinks, digests, wears clothes, tinkles the piano, dances, sings, handles a golfclub, submits to sex, bears a child without the smallest notion of anatomy, turns from the whole thing disgusted, and probably bears no more. Whose fault? Not hers. They do not teach mothercraft or physiology in finishing schools for gentlemen's daughters, and it is no part of the duty of gentlemen's wives to reproduce their kind. Perhaps there is comfort in that.

A great many parents, however, would tell us that they gave their daughters a good and liberal education in such schools as were available, good ordinary boarding and day-schools which have sprung up during the last fifty years in response to the feminist propaganda. Then we have the working woman, who has shared with her brothers in what education is permitted to trickle through the elementary schools. It must not be forgotten that this ends at fourteen.

Is there something wrong with this education of women, and if so, what? I think we must judge that there is. The reason lies in the sense of inferiority bred in women by so much oppression, and the natural result that their chief aim as they struggled upwards was to prove that in all respects they were just as good as men. The second aim was to prove that they could jolly well do without them. In exactly the same way the worker, rising in the social scale, seeks to prove himself a *bourgeois*. Both efforts are mistaken. Each class and sex has that to give to the common stock of achievement, knowledge, thought, which it alone can give, and robs itself and the community by inferior imitation. The feminist movement, like one dissentient voice in an excited public meeting, was querulous, hysterical, uncertain of itself. It dared not cry out that women had bodies. Its one hope of success was to prove that women had minds. And it was right in this, that the primary fact about men and women is not that they are two sexes apart, but that they are human beings and as such should share all knowledge in the world and make it the basis of their partnership and the rearing of their children.

Many an ardent feminist spinster in a girls' secondary school has sighed over the state of public opinion which forced her to drive her girls' minds along channels for which they were not always suited, that they might do well at college and show that women could surpass the men. Many another, well drilled by a mother or tradition in ideals of feminine virtue, gloried in the sexless learned women she was creating and in the thought that one day they would force those savage, lustful men to conform to the ideals which they set up for women. Why blame her? Lay the blame where it is due. It will be but a just retribution for that lustful male and his ideal of feminine virtue if one day, in a world full of prohibitions, he finds himself forced to kneel before the Mumbo-Jumbo[4] he himself built up to terrify his wives and daughters to submission.

Feminist ideals of education, then, had the defect that they did in a certain measure deny sex, or ignore it. The feminists had a pathetic hope that by so doing they would convince the dominant male that a woman might be learned and yet remain a lady. But I wish to emphasize the fact that this feature has belonged to all education of women, especially of ladies, from time immemorial, and it is, therefore, unbecoming in a male, whether young or old, to use this as a cause for reproach to our sex. We went as far as we dared with an eye to male hostility. Young feminists to-day would be the first to admit that it would probably have paid us to go further. There never has been a period when education has trained women for the possibility of motherhood, and it is time that such training was begun. There never was a period when the education of women was completely honest, and it is time that training was begun. What knowledge is of more vital importance to women than anatomy and physiology? They were allowed it if they were to be doctors, and then only with caution. Turning casually the pages of a book on anatomy in a girls' secondary school library, I found the diagrams connected with sex and maternity carefully stuck fast. What is more calculated to inspire prying and prurience? We have no right to blame young women for shirking marriage, sex, or motherhood, or for moulding their figures on boyish lines, when we carefully treat them as boys and withhold from them as long as we can all knowledge of the difference of their physique and possibly of their destiny. I have no wish to go back on the great achievements of feminism, or to drive women from the professions in which they have a just right to be employed. I want to break down the last barriers. Artemis is slim and bold; Athene is stately. We have done well to worship at their shrines.

But the call of Demeter the Fruitful is insistent. If we would add to the achievements of those who came before us, let us freely admit that we have but been playing mock modesty, and that to us the body is no mere box to hold the mind, but a temple of delight and ecstasy: a temple to hold the future if we will. To me the important task of modern feminism is to accept and proclaim sex; to bury for ever the lie that has too long corrupted our society – the lie that the body is a hindrance to the mind, and sex a necessary evil to be endured for the perpetuation of our race. To understand sex – to bring to it dignity and beauty and knowledge born of science, in place of brute instinct and squalor – that is the bridge that will span the breach between Jason and Medea.

Chapter III

ASPASIA

The Younger Feminists

While we have admitted that the first aim of the feminist movement was to open to women the stores of learning, to develop their minds and to teach them to think, and that no attempt was made to handle the problem of sex, it is not quite fair to say that even early feminism has consistently denied or despised the body. The schools and colleges made it their business to give to women opportunites for physical development, for open-air exercise, swimming, tennis, hockey, lacrosse. The Victorian young woman learnt gradually to be ashamed of her tiny waist and fat hips. She learnt that a healthy appetite[5] as well became a young woman as a young man, gave up her snacks in private and did justice to good meals taken at proper intervals. Quietly, and without mention of the fatal word 'sex,' the spinster feminists, by emphasis on health and vigour, built up a generation of young women who were to be frank about desires besides eating and drinking.

I cannot see what is the matter with our figures. Steel rods and rubber are more modern materials than oak beams and pink plaster. Neither we nor our modern lovers admire the opulent Venuses, indolent and rose-embowered, who adorned the ceilings of old-fashioned ballrooms. They were stupid, self-indulgent creatures, not even good mothers, whatever the sentimental elderly gentlemen in their top-hats and whiskers may have to say. What is a good mother we will discuss in a later chapter, but for the present it is enough to say that more dangerous childbirths are due to narrow pelves caused by rickets than to hips contracted by the corsets of vanity. Let the doctors turn socialist and feed the poor, instead of spending their time lamenting the inadequacy for childbirth of a few fashionable women who don't very much matter. Middle- and upper-class girls nowadays – and most working-class girls, too – go corsetless up to maturity. They do gymnastic exercises, and dances that give suppleness to the body. They swim and they play out of doors. Those who are rich enough to be adequately fed are graceful and active as kittens, and as healthy. By the time adolescence brings, as it always does, a few years of intensive sex-vanity, the corset can do very little harm. The muscular little body does not tolerate it stiff, or very tight, and the bones are well grown. The mystery of feminine dress helps the appearance of slimness. There are few clothes, and no lumpy gathers. Beneath that boyish outline are firm little breasts, clean arching hips, abdominal curves and thighs, lovely as anything the Venus of Milo has to show.

Artemis fashioned this modern woman. That is admitted. Has Artemis her vows?

I'm afraid for once we have to admit that the Bishops are right. In spite of everything the Church can do, in spite of an education committed, so far as the authorities can control it, to sour or religious spinsters, the modern young woman is not very moral. It is a pathetic picture which the author of *Lysistrata* had drawn for us, of sexless beings going to and fro in tube and bus like shuttles in a machine to dull work robbed of all joy, earning their livelihood and turning their backs on man in response to feminist propaganda. Man, the enemy – to be defeated in his own professions, to be repelled in every onslaught upon feminine virtue: I wonder? I would hazard a guess that, relatively to the population, fewer women retain their virginity till death than in the Victorian period or the Middle Ages. In all probability it is sex, not sexlessness, which makes women cling so tenaciously to the right to earn their living. Marriage brings a jealous intolerant husband, children, prying and impertinent neighbours – degraded and humiliating slavery for the vast majority of women. Thirty shillings a week and typing or working in a shop, a still tongue, or a toss of the head and the assertion that independence is the best; and, in the background a lover with whom somehow evenings are spent – a lover who has no claim and cannot tyrannize. A lover, perhaps, who pleads to become a husband, but has no chance unless his income is good or secure. Marriage would change him: Aspasia knows it. Marriage would also rob her of that thirty shillings a week, which alone stands between her and the abyss of primeval submission. Or else Aspasia teaches in a school or college. She is a skilled teacher, devoted to her work and pupils. She may be a Research Fellow in some difficult branch of learning which is to her the very breath of life. She may be a doctor in the public service, tending and advising mothers and children. She is lovely, vital, creative. Man approaches. There are holidays of delight and secret dread of the scandal which will end the work Aspasia loves – or marriage and the certainty of that end at once. 'Choose,' say the Bishops and the school-managers (often the same thing); 'choose,' say the public authorities who support the Church and rather wish women would get out of this indelicate profession of surgery and medicine; 'choose between love and duty to the male and service to the community.' This is not feminism – feminists have fought it persistently – it is medieval Christianity. It presents a choice between physical pleasure and service to the mind or soul; it upholds the time-honoured theory that renunciation of the world, the flesh, and the devil is the path to duty and salvation. I am fully aware of all the arguments about economic pressure, the primary right of married men to work, the awful situation of their dependent children and their wives. None of this is fundamental, and the jealous male knows it. 'Divide to conquer' is the principle in dealing with trade unions; it works equally well in the feminist struggle. Persuade the single women that the married woman is an unfair competitor,[6] terrify them so far as you can into believing that to succumb to sex is something unbecoming and disgraceful and punishable with misery everlasting, whether in marriage or outside it, and you can prevent the women combining against you.

But not if Aspasia will speak. If she but would, and put an end to this lie for ever. She could tell us how, especially during the years of war, young women took the last step towards feminine emancipation by admitting to themselves and their lovers the mutual nature of sex-love between man and woman. It sounds a platitude, but is, in fact, a revolution.

Strange to say, the nearness of death from enemy bombs or enemy fire did not intensify the thought of holiness and heaven. It made the little footrules to measure morality look absurd; it mocked the emptiness of female virtue. While poverty and parents forbade the certainty of marriage, with nothing but instability and death around them, our modern Aspasias took the love of man and gave the love of woman, and found this union, free and full on either side, the most priceless gift the immortal gods can bestow. There is nothing new in this, the moralist will say – it is just wickedness. Yes, there is this that is new: that, though these younger women may be driven from fear of starvation to the outward acceptance of old codes and conventions, inwardly they know they have done no wrong and will not admit a conviction of sin. Sex, even without children and without marriage, is to them a thing of dignity, beauty, and delight. All Puritans – and most males so long as they can remember – have tried to persuade women that their part in sex is pregnancy and childbirth, and not momentary delight. As well tell a man his part is the hunting and skinning of animals for food and clothing. To enjoy and admit we enjoy, without terror or regret, is an achievement in honesty. We will go further and say that polygamy, proffered by the male as a solution to our sexless lives, is no solution at all when we are polyandrous. It is useless to go on pretending, as both sexes do, about this question. The plain truth is that there are as many types of lover among women of all classes as among men, and that nothing but honesty and freedom will make instinctive satisfaction possible for all. Grant each man and woman the right to seek his or her own solution without fear of public censure. Moral questions of this kind cannot be decided by some abstract rule. It would not be wrong for a man to have six wives, provided he and they all found mutual happiness in that arrangement; nor for a woman to have six husbands and a child by each, if she and they found such a life satisfactory. The wrong lies in rules that are barriers between human beings who would otherwise reach a fuller and more intense understanding of one another. And any man or woman of intelligence and vitality can testify that to have known each other as lovers is to have completed mental and spiritual, as well as physical, understanding, and to have permanently enriched each other's lives, capacities, energies, imaginations. There is no need to make these divisions into mind and body. There is no difference. A way of walking, laughter, thoughts spoken or written, gestures of love or anger, colour and light of eyes or hair – these are the human being, man or woman. It is thus that modern individuals think of one another. When we think so, it seems absurd to argue whether or no love between man and woman should stop short of a certain kind of physical expression. It is useless to say that a mental exchange is sufficient. On the contrary, lovers know that it is through sexual understanding they best apprehend the quality of each other's minds. It is equally futile to argue that woman is cheated of her full rights if children do not result. That is not true.

It is said that modern human beings, by dint of not valuing the body, are physically degenerate and lose the finest ecstasies of love. Their digestions are poor, we are told, their breath foul, their teeth bad. Was love more delightful, then, in the old days when baths were unknown, when 'sweet breath' in a woman was so rare as to be sung by poets, and the reek of stale sweat was barely stifled by a strong perfume? John Donne wrote verse to the flea he saw nestling in his lady's bosom. There is scarcely a fine gentleman to-day who could face the prospect of making love to one of the fine ladies of the past six or seven hundred years in Europe, if she could be presented to him just as she was to her contemporary lovers. It is true that neither vermin, filth, nor squalor – being equal for both – can stay the passion of sex whether now or in the past, but I do not believe in the theory that the rougher our physique the more intense our bodily delights. Health, to be sure, is essential; but health is to be secured in the modern world, not by a return to savagery, but by the use of intelligence. I believe the bodies of young people of to-day to whom fair opportunities have been given are more healthy within and without than they were in past times. And I believe that the disappearance of religious and moral dualism between mind and matter – not by an oppressive victory of either, neither by rational and moral control, nor by abandonment to sensual materialism, but by a better understanding of psychology and physiology based on the discoveries of physical science – is bringing to the whole of life, but especially to sex-love, maternity, the rearing and education of children, joy and rapture and promise surpassing anything known to the purely instinctive life of the past. Of course we are bewildered. Civilization without decay is at last a possibility. Let us have knowledge and patience: blaspheming and violence will ruin all.

It is for modern women and for men who can understand the problem to make an end to secrecy, shame, and starvation where sex is concerned. There has been a good deal of freedom in action, but less boldness in speech, because of the heavy penalties involved. For some women speech is impossible; those who are secure must fight their battle. How old and proper people love a vigorous and god-like young male! How they look askance upon, brow-beat, and bully his equivalent in the opposite sex! Here is a community for ever stifling their voices in education and public life; then turning and rending the submissive residue for being what years of intimidation have made them. Let them marry, you say, and make a success of that and their children. That would be well enough but for the taboos and disabilities with which marriage is surrounded. Feminism led women away from the home that they might return armed and unsubdued to make marriage tolerable. Women who have been free remember the horror of the approach to marriage: a barrier for most of us to free public activity; a life-long contract only to be broken in disgrace and public disgust; aunts, uncles, social duties that exasperate and are totally unnecessary; the common view that henceforward husband and wife are one and indivisible, and the wife for ever to be burdened with her husband's duties and affairs; looks of surprise and reproach if we enjoy other male society; constraint in the manner of men formerly our friends; income, if we have any or can still earn, taxed as a part of our husband's; children, which, had we had them illegitimate, would have been our own but now are our husband's; worst of all, the looks and smiles from silly women broken in to slavery, congratulating us on having done well and made ourselves secure for life.

Let no one think this is petulant abuse. It is the accumulation of these details and the pressure of public opinion which gradually destroy the nerve and independent judgment of married women who, in their free state, have been brilliant and remarkable. It is the fact that by marriage, we conform and place ourselves in a line with millions of others whose view of what we have done is entirely foreign to our own. As a Labour Minister is corrupted by Court dress, so is a free woman by the marriage-contract. Nothing but our desire for children would make us endure it. We to whom the mutual nature of sex-love is sacred, to whom a partnerhsip involving children is of equal dignity on both sides, to whom the surrender of our whole being in love is a free gift – the highest we can bestow; who would neither bind ourselves nor others where love is non-existent; we must submit to a contract based on rights of property and possession, buying and selling of our bodies; a law whose conception of conjugal wrongs is sin, punishment, and just revenge; and a Church whose utmost concession is to bid us 'serve' instead of 'obey' our husbands. Build, O Aspasia, a trade union of lovers to conquer the world, and cry aloud that feminism is nowhere so much needed as in the home.

Chapter IV

HECUBA

Feminist Mothers

So far I have refrained from any detailed discussion of modern women and maternity because it is still necessary to make it clear that a full life of activity for women is perfectly possible and permissible without it. I am quite aware that certain religious people assert as a moral principle that the purpose of sex-love is not mutual enjoyment but the perpetuation of the race. I am also aware that militarists enjoin on women the necessity of marriage and large families as a patriotic duty. Further, certain doctors have gone out of their way to try to prove that the use of contraceptives is contrary to health and nature. These same people, we may note, have no aversion from the wearing by women of internal remedial rubber supports for months on end nor to patching up with silver, papier mâché, and other foreign materials, the insides and outsides of human beings mutilated in the natural and healthy pursuit called war. I am not concerned with the morals of convention or superstition, but with the morals of experience. It is the experience of modern women that sex is an instinctive need to them as it is to men, and further that the prevention of conception brings to them no loss of poise, health, or happiness. On the contrary, when once they embark on the task of maternity, contraception is a blessed safeguard to health and recovery in the periods of rest between pregnancies. I am not going to deny that the most perfect delight known to human beings is the completely reckless, mutually adoring union of two people of vitality and intelligence who hope to create another human being as a constant reminder of the beauty of that moment. But many considerations, which we shall discuss, forbid a yearly child. I read recently in an article by G. K. Chesterton, that sex without gestation and parturition is like blowing the trumpets and waving the flags without doing any of the fighting. From a woman such words, though displaying inexperience, might come with dignity; from a man they are an unforgivable, intolerable insult. What is man's part in sex but a perpetual waving of flags and blowing of trumpets and avoidance of the fighting? The vast majority of men are not even tender or kindly to their pregnant or nursing wives, nor will they give help or consideration to the care of their young children.

A revolt against motherhood under present conditions is not surprising, nor is it entirely regrettable. There are quite a number of women whose minds and bodies are not fitted or have not been fitted by their upbringing and education to produce and care for children. This is a source of distress to many people, who, as was suggested earlier, did not think of it at the right moment, when the education of women in public and private schools was being developed. Even now these same people stand in the way of the surest remedy: which is to teach science, physiology, and the beauty of sex and maternity to boys and girls at an early age. The London County Council, many of whom are certainly distressed beyond measure at the falling birth-rate and the discontent and irresponsibility of modern young people, have just, in consultation with suitably selected moral headmasters and mistresses, turned down the suggestion of sexteaching in elementary and secondary schools. We are always told that boys and girls of all classes nowadays acquire this knowledge easily for themselves, but the mere knowledge is not the only thing to the adolescent mind. Things not spoken of by parents or teachers, things dealt with in hushed voices by moral and spiritual leaders, surrounded by cant and humbug and false sentiment, are bound to be thought nasty by mild young people and to provide ribald laughter for the obstreperous.

This is not to say that sex-information should be given in a spirit of evangelical solemnity and exhortation, nor even of soft sentimentality. All that is needed is lessons in physiology, taught as a matter of course, as botany or nature-study are often taught; and then explanations to boys of the working of their bodies, how to keep them in health, how not to dissipate and destroy their energies too soon. Further, they should be told that woman is neither a chattel nor a servant, nor even inferior, but a partner in joy as in the business of life; that there is no question or difficulty, public or private, which cannot be brought to her for discussion and judgment; and that she has a right to share in all decisions affecting a joint life, children, money, and the conduct of affairs of State. To girls in the same way could be explained the physical changes of puberty, marriage, and maternity, how the child grows, what food and care the mother, and afterwards the baby, will need. There is nothing in this too difficult or shocking to young or adolescent minds. So many of us can remember the secret conclaves with our friends when we puzzled out and pieced together what scraps of information we could glean, awakening instinct darkly supplementing this knowledge. Some of us can remember, perhaps, having noticed obscene writing on school-walls, instantly reported by shocked prefects, instantly effaced by school-mistresses with an awful and portentous gravity which made us feel we had stumbled on the brink of a secret of incredible wickedness and horror. One straightforward lecture of concise information could have dispelled lurking mystery once and for all and imparted a sense of magic and wonder and ambition. Some of the more fortunate of us, through study in libraries and dreaming over poems, created for ourselves a finer attitude. With no teaching other than that we might find someone who would marry us some day, and that marriage was an excellent destiny even for educated women, and with no belief in any of the moral taboos current around us, some of us can none the less remember the pride of caring for the body, safeguarding health and looks, avoiding excess, severe strain, and overwork, because we cherished our dreams of the children that our bodies were to make – not ordinary children, of course not: Promethean creatures, endowed with every gift that mortal man could steal from the jealous gods, strong, beautiful, intelligent, and bold – kings and conquerors, not of their fellow-creatures but of nature and the mystery of the world. There is not a woman, unless completely warped by early training, in whom such dreams and visions will not stir if we try to wake them. If not, then let her pass: we do not need her to perpetuate the race. And do not trick her into motherhood by false sentiment and information, or by withholding from her the means to protect herself if she is not fully resolved upon bearing a child.

We want better reasons for having children than not knowing how to prevent them. Nor should we represent motherhood as something so common and easy that everyone can go through it without harm or suffering and rear her children competently and well. Without arousing dread or horror, we should tell young women frankly the pain and agony of childbirth, and the anxiety and griefs which are the fate of every woman who is a mother by choice and therefore loves her children. Nothing whatever is to be gained by driving the timorous and weak by lies or compulsion into pain which they will resent and responsibility which they will evade. Everything is to be gained by training a woman in knowledge, courage, and physical strength, and leaving it then to her own instinct and her mind to tell her that to create new human beings is worth the discomfort and the suffering which she must necessarily undergo. Those in whom the courage to create survives when choice is free and all the facts are known are those best fitted to bring children into the world, and breed in them eagerness and intrepidity. The others will only pass on fear and distaste for life from which individuals and the community suffer far too much already.[7]

I do not mean by this that we should, scorning the aid of science, return to natural childbirth, and let its pangs scare off the weaklings and the cowards. In this matter the charges of our critics are conflicting. They condemn us for having sought the aid of science to mitigate our suffering, and in the same breath tell us that a return to natural child-bed will bring back a primitive exhilaration and freedom from pain lost for thousands of years. I do not believe that for any comparatively civilized race, any race really worthy the name of man, childbirth has ever been painless. The upright position, held by eighteenth-century divines to be a source of pride in man, was the first injustice to women. Nor do I believe that the sufferings of modern women are any worse or their confinements any more difficult than those of women in the past. They are more closely observed and the difficulties known, and, where skill is available, the dangerous ones are less likely to be fatal. In the past the fragile woman died, or continued ailing, unobserved by a doctor and afraid to complain. People who live and breed in a state of nature are by no means so healthy and vigorous as our modern Rousseaus would have us believe: more children die than survive, and those who are left have physical defects and deformities which could have been remedied by knowledge and care. These and the ravages of smallpox and other diseases, and the deformities due to the natural accidents of life unmitigated by medical care, produce far more ugliness than the mark of an obstetric instrument on temple or forehead. Then, again, youth passes more quickly. The men and women we see in modern life, still reasonably young and fresh with rounded faces and teeth stopped or supplemented by art, would in a more primitive community be dead, or else crouching useless and despised, toothless and with sunken cheeks by the fireside of their sons and daughters.

Decay and pain belong to nature. To arrest the one and mitigate the other has been the task which the sciences that deal in physiology have set themselves. Remedial at first, they pass on to the stage of prevention. Already the principle of intelligent medicine is to strengthen what is weak in the body by nourishment and exercise rather than provide artificial substitutes. Paralysed limbs return to life; women retain their teeth white and strong through several pregnancies. This is not done by a return to nature, but by an increase in civilization and knowledge. In that way our very landscapes have been formed. We prune, we nourish the soil, we cross-breed our plants. The vegetables upon which the enthusiast for nature urges us to live are the product of science and artifice: thousands of years of cultivation, nitrates from Chile, skill of the experimenter, skill of the gardener's hand. The same is true of the animals we breed for meat, eggs, or milk supply. Agriculture and stock-breeding seem natural to us – they were not natural in the distant past. As regards the human body, to me at least it seems that we are now beginning to approach the right attitude. There was more dosing and doctoring of petty ailments among intelligent people in the last century. To-day we try to learn how best to live in order that such ailments may not occur, and substitute a well-balanced diet for aids to digestion and the normal functioning of our bodies. We do the same in rearing our children. And this attitude would become more general if those who rule us, Press, Church, rich men and politicians, would consider it really important that every man, woman, and child in the State should have health and happiness, and therefore supply broadcast the necessary rules of life and sufficient of healthy and staple foods for all, in place of advertisement of quack remedies and patent substitutes prepared by profiteers.

To return to the application of science and nature to maternity. A special sentimentality and superstition inherited from the completely savage periods of history cling about this, as about sex. The avoidance of suffering in childbirth is taboo in the Japanese moral code, as it was until recently in Christian morals. Religion has persisted in regarding the female body as unclean when engaged in its most important functions, and purifying it afterwards by special prayers to the Deity.[8] We find this savagery current in Judaism[9] as in Christianity, together with an exhortation to be fruitful and multiply, and therefore to pass through shame and uncleanness as often as we can. It was thought a horror and an outrage when chloroform was used to help us. It is a still greater horror when means are discovered of not having children at all. To this day most doctors and dentists refuse to give an anaesthetic and draw a rotten tooth which is wearing down a pregnant mother's strength by sleepless nights and days of agony. Yet this can be done with reasonable care and skill. Behind all this there is the mystic belief that somehow or other nature does the work best unaided and unhindered; and this mysticism is rooted in a savage taboo. Life is, indeed, so pertinacious that somehow some of us will survive whatever we do, but this does not seem to me an adequate attitude for the rational mother.

The truth is that it is not desired or expected that mothers should be rational. Maternal instinct is so wonderful, maternal devotion so sublime, cry our sentimental brutes. Whatever we may have known of life and the outside world, it is still expected in modern times that, once married, we shall descend into a morass of instinct and ignorance from which we shall never, if the male and the vindictively-minded spinster can prevent it, emerge again. We are privileged, so we are told, in that we may bear each year a child for the State, rock the cradle, wash, mend, and make, pass on the lore of housekeeping and infant-care to our daughters just as we received it from our mothers. It is such a beautiful picture: a pity it is entirely false. The old-fashioned mother had no lore, and her instinct was inadequate. She succeeded by luck rather than by knowledge. She adored, or disciplined; she killed by kindness or by severity and neglect. She would coddle when she should have hardened, harden when she should have coddled; she would over-feed and under-feed, or give the wrong kind of food. Since it has been the fashion for women to have minds, the books for mothers have become more scientific and our intelligent inquiries have been met by research and more adequate replies. Every mother with any intelligence who has reared one or more children through the first year of life and up to five years of age would admit nowadays that scientific knowledge was of more service to her than all the instinct and adoration at her command. Indeed, I believe the so-called maternal instinct in handling and understanding babies consists of habit almost imperceptibly learnt in tending the first, blossoming into a smooth instinctive unity with the coming of the second. The fashionable mother, said to be devoid of maternal instinct because she neglects her child, has simply not learnt it, because necessity does not compel her to practical duties. This is even true, though less so, of well-to-do mothers who feed their babies at the breast.

People will persist in imagining that uncivilized women were always able to feed their children in natural fashion. Very often they were obliged to seek the help of another mother, and, when that was not forthcoming, the baby died. It is quite true that our adaptation to modern conditions of life, nerve-stress, combined with overwork for women in towns and industrial districts, has caused breast-feeding to be less common than it was in the past. But here again the way of life is not back to nature, which is impossible because we cannot at a blow destroy industrialism and the towns – but onwards, to greater knowledge. Instead of bullying the mothers and telling them it is wicked not to feed their babies at the breast, let them know how, by pre-natal care of health and strength, by diet, by deliberate nerve-control, they can feed their babies with comfort and delight and without detriment to their health and the work which they must necessarily do – or even to their beauty. Here again, if choice is free and the child therefore ardently desired, there is more chance of success with breast-feeding. And knowledge of the chemical constituents of cow's milk and patent foods as compared with human milk is more likely to induce the modern mother to suckle her child than volumes of abuse or sentimental twaddle.

Then as to the hygiene of pregnancy. Could our mothers have taught us about the different food-values, about protein, hydro-carbonates, calcium from the green foods for teeth and bones, avoidance of too many albuminous foods? Knowledge of what diet can do to help us in pregnancy and our children in early youth is in its infancy, but it is there, none the less. Shall we fling it aside and return to pure instinct? What massage and remedial exercises have taught can be applied to our bodies during pregnancy and after childbirth. It is probable that closer study of the functions of the muscles of the back and the abdomen would enable us to teach women to exercise and control them in a way that would make childbirth almost painless, and the recovery of poise and activity afterwards more rapid and more thorough. Under present conditions, muscles that are often too rigid or too feeble expand and never recover their tone; others – the back muscles, it may be – go out of use temporarily and similarly do not recover. In the middle-class woman laziness is often the cause of difficult confinements and poor recovery of the figure; in the working mother a too speedy return to work which is too hard and does not exercise the body harmoniously; in both the ignorance which leads to wrong kinds of nourishment during pregnancy, and fear of doing harm to the child which leads to rigid and over-careful movement, are responsible for a good many troubles. Psychological effects may be serious. Most women develop during pregnancy sensitiveness and a timidity protective to the child. From this the very fertile mother has no opportunity to recover. Hence many of the silly old ladies who cannot cross roads unaided by a policeman. With birth-control, in two years a determined mother can completely restore her nerve, her joy in life, and her full muscular powers.

The author of *Lysistrata* suggests that by diet we may produce thin babies and therefore have easier confinements. This may be true, but knowledge is imperfect, and the experience of some mothers goes to show that a light diet, with much green food, while keeping the mother slim and supple, produces a plump 8 to 9 lbs. baby. Starchy foods, on the contrary, which seem to keep the baby slim, mean for the mother uncomfortable corpulence and lessened muscular vigour. I think the size of our babies is perhaps not so much under our control as many might wish to suggest. Heredity enters in. Children sometimes have large fathers. The sheep-breeder knows that he dare not mate certain larger types of rams with small-made ewes.

In all these problems, however, it is the frankness and intelligence which feminism has made possible for women which will bring solution and progress, rather than a return to the unguided instincts of our forefathers. The lore of motherhood is a science which is now beginning, but it is not following the lines which convention and the moralists expect. It defies sentiment, ridicules unnecessary and unintelligent sacrifice, is not content to suffer, but makes demands. It begins with birth-control, which to many seems the negation of motherhood, but which to the creative mother is the keystone of her work.

Suppose we have educated our young women sanely about physical matters, as suggested earlier in this chapter. As they reach the age of maturity and activity, what will they find? If they are middle- or upper-class, an existence that is not too intolerable. Feminism has won for them the right of entry to most professions and, provided they are fairly able, they can get work. None the less, it must be admitted that the years since the War have borne hardly upon wage-earning women of all classes. The lack of sexual freedom is a terrible burden, but the remedy ultimately lies in their own hands.

Life in marriage still offers reasonable comfort and good food for man and wife and two or three children. But late marriages, from the lack of opportunity for men and the expense of living, cause girls' young bodies to be worn with longing unless they are bold enough to follow our modern Aspasias. This waiting to marry is a real danger to young women's health which conventional, unimaginative people refuse to face. It produces nervous disorders bordering at times on insanity.

As regards the care of her body in pregnancy and childbirth, and the feeding of her children, the middle-class mother is in a position to carry out what modern science has to teach. She cannot have a large family, it is true, and the cry goes up on all sides that it is very hard for the middle-classes to pay for the proper education of their children.[10] The best stocks are being penalized and extinguished, so we are told. This is part of a much bigger problem, and a problem that involves the class-war. All ambitious mothers, from miners' wives to the aristocracy, would like to breed the fine types who receive a thorough education and then enter one of the intellectual professions. Obviously this cannot be. And, given equal ability in two children of different classes of life, there is no just reason for driving the worker's child, who has less good food and conditions and is therefore less fitted to stand the strain, through the worry of the scholarship system, whilst the other child's path is made smooth to a ruling position. Man for man, woman for woman, the workers would be the equals of the middle-class in strength and ability, given the same nourishment, comfort and training. In actual fact, the middle-class is perpetually being replenished in one generation, or two at most, from below. Middle-class fathers and mothers have no right to claim the privilege of a large family unless their children, if they are strong but not clever, are prepared to work the railways or dig coal in the mines. Professional people, scientists, artists, research workers, pure mathematicians, as well as skilled engineers, are, indeed, the salt of the earth, and the community that fails to produce them and give them scope is doomed in this modern world. But they are supported by manual labour, and it cannot be denied that their number cannot be indefinitely extended except by an increase of productivity and wealth. A more equal system of society will diminish drudgery and make it possible for all to have a fine development of intelligence and understanding, whatever the work on which they are employed.

Feminism in the mother has led us far from maternity. That is what it is bound to do. The working mother today looks straight from her kitchen, if she is lucky enough to have one, on to one of the most complex situations in history. And the intelligent ones are not blind to the situation. That is why I suggested that, though middle-class feminism has conquered the professions, the feminism of working mothers might bring a new and powerful contribution to our work.

The life of the working woman who intends maternity is becoming well-nigh impossible, and she knows it. When she has found a husband the community denies them a decent house. Possibly they find one room or two at an exorbitant rent, with no water and a grate unsuited for cooking. There are no restaurants at which the pair can afford to feed. Therefore they exist on partially or casually-cooked food, innutritious bread, and food from tins. Things may not be so bad if the wife can go on with work at a mill and get food that is fairly good at the canteen, her wages helping the meals taken at home.

The coming of a baby too often means a search for another lodging. The Bishops and the Generals like babies, but landladies don't. Another room is found, perhaps. The mother works till the last moment, has a difficult confinement and inadequate attention, and gets up too soon. It is not easier for her than for a delicately-nurtured woman, and it is not less painful. Probably it is worse, because the working mother has from birth been underfed and has weaknesses and deformities – a contracted pelvis, perhaps – that a woman well-fed and cared for escapes. Then it goes on, baby after baby up to ten and eleven,[11] always in one room and no more money coming in. The mother works whenever she can to help keep the family. Frequently she is cursed or beaten by her husband for her fertility. Should the husband die, she must work continually and harder or send her children to the workhouse. In the opinion of the Bishops, she deserves the 'stigma of the Poor Law,' and, in the opinion of all right-thinking people, anything done for her by individuals or the State is in the nature of a charity.

If I but had the eloquence of Hecuba mourning her slaughtered sons! The crime of war is bad enough: this butchery of hope and promise and human lives is one so black that the heart and mind of every woman who has borne a child should revolt against it until it is tolerated no more. It is easy to escape into an aristocratic theory of society. It has been done before, and ends in the guillotine. These working mothers are the people who must be lied to and terrified by bogies for fear that they use their votes to help themselves. And it is they who, when they sit in conference, demand of the State the right to stem the tide of children, to endow mothers, to pension widows, to teach and tend maternity and ensure rest for pregnant and nursing women; to see that houses and schools are built, and to control and purify the food-supply. Here is the most serious problem for the mothers, and one which the middle-class politician does not touch, because for the middle-class pure and fresh food is almost always obtainable. It is for the working mother to tackle those tins. She cannot now destroy industrialism, which dragged her work and her after it to the mill; but she can claim her right to control it in the name of life and the destiny of her children. Control of the population is essential to solving the food-problem and improving national health. Women in small houses know it. They know, moreover, that contraceptives are better than infanticide and war. The survival of the fittest is a false doctrine in child-bearing as in fighting. Every child which starts with a reasonably good constitution can, by the right care up to one year and food up to five, grow up to be strong and well. And, if the weak and unhealthy are discouraged from breeding and healthy mothers given proper care, great improvements are possible. Poor food and over-crowding are the ladder down which we go to mental deficiency and ultimate complete feebleness of mind.[12] If we cared for life, the best food would by law go to the pregnant and nursing mothers instead of, as at present, to clubs for fat old gentlemen and the frequenters of palatial hotels. It is probable that at present we do not produce enough milk, or produce and import enough butter and eggs to distribute adequately to all.[13] But, by stabilizing or decreasing our population, and by co-operation, intensive culture and control of marketing abroad and of marketing and purity at home, we could see to it that everybody had enough and that what they had was really good.

To feed an industrial population in a small island is a peculiar and special problem and one demanding expert care and advice. Food must come long distances and must 'keep.' Hence the preservatives and tins and the need to be watchful beyond measure against poisoning and the loss of what is vital to our well-being. With research, the problem would be easy; but we must make it clear that it is important. Science would easily enable us to produce more from the soil, and, as regards the food of mothers, since the assimilation of extra minerals, salts, etc., in their natural state is not always satisfactory or easy during pregnancy, we might find ways of growing food, through treatment of the soil, to provide for the special needs of their condition.

What then must feminist mothers demand? The right first of all to the recognition of their work – the most dangerous of all trades and the most neglected and despised. They should ask for endowment from the community. This is opposed by many on the ground that fathers delight to support their children, and it is they who should claim from the community an adequate family-wage. But, after all, it is the mother who bears and tends the child, and, although many women receive the whole of their husbands' wages, others must fight a humiliating battle against drink and tobacco for the wherewithal to build their children's bodies. This struggle is exemplified on a large scale in the spending of State revenue, most of which goes on armaments and the forces of destruction, and an infinitesimal portion to aid and support life. If Jason cannot give up his murderous play-things, let him have neither sons to destroy nor daughters to drag through misery. His children shall never be conceived. I have indicated that this is happening already, not as a deliberate revolt, but as a counsel of despair in a world which offers no hope, no joy, and no opportunity to the young.

The mother has a right to demand two years' rest

between pregnancies; and the right to decide the number of her children. For some the call of motherhood is insistent and its charm grows with experience; they would be good mothers and might well have large families. They could help others by superintending nursery-schools in which children from one to five years might have their important meal of the day. But it is imperative that the woman who has children should not be shut out from public life. The ideal would be for a woman to continue her education at least till eighteen, have the first child at twenty-four, then perhaps three others at two-year intervals. This assumes that large numbers of women do not choose to breed. At thirty-five every mother of four children would, in a community of good schools, convenient houses, and well-run restaurants, be free again to take part in public life. It does not follow that she would be separated from her children: they would go to day-schools. But the mother would do the work for which she was best fitted in school,[14] kitchen, hospital, shop, mill, or Parliament. In this way her opinion would count, and her attitude to life help to permeate the community, which is otherwise left to be guided by the outlook of the single woman and the male. Problems of unemployment and competition due to married women's work are really questions of population pressure, muddled thinking, and bad organization. To discuss all this in close detail is hardly within the scope of this book.

In conclusion, it may be said that the community should never, except on the strongest grounds, deny parenthood to man or woman. Therefore marriages which after two years did not result in a child should be dissoluble at the wish of either party to the contract. This, apart from all other reasons for which the cancelling of marriage should be allowed. Partnership in marriage should in effect be regarded as a partnership for parenthood, and as such should not be entered upon lightly.

Chapter V

JASON AND ADMETUS
Men

Before we pass on to an attempt at a summary and conclusion of the argument, it may be as well to re-state briefly what is the matter with men. Certainly they are not such fierce tyrants as when first we fought them; certainly they have some grounds to complain of the feminine arrogance which, not content with proving equality, wants to go on and prove women the superior sex. We might, on grounds of science perhaps, advance this claim, urging that, since a female being needs one more chromosome for its creation than a male, it must, therefore, be of higher importance. Should we do so, and seek to live alone on the planet, producing our children by parthenogenesis, our pride would be doomed to a fall. Such children, there is reason to believe, would all be males. At least, that is what happens when the experiment is tried by sea-urchins. Men, on the other hand, like to pretend that our assumption of intelligence and independence is but a momentary spurt in a race which must end in masculine victory and feminine submission. They admit that the great development of our freedom in body and mind has given us a serious advantage, and the more discerning among them urge their fellows to press on and catch us up. Others trundle the golden apples beseechingly, but still Atalanta runs.

I believe it to be true that the education and outlook of men is more old-fashioned than that of women reared in the freedom of feminist traditions. Men have not yet realized how women's outlook is changing, nor attempted very seriously to adapt themselves to the change. They will do so, of a certainty; for, true as it may be that above all desires in woman is that to be pleasing to men, it is still truer that the desire of desires in man is to be pleasing to women. I believe that

Puritanism or asceticism, of which they accuse us, is very strong in them. One of the compliments or insults that has been hurled during the sex-war is that the feminine mind is pervaded by the physical harmony of the feminine body. One may perhaps retort that the dualism of mind and matter is a very masculine philosophy; and one which, moreover, men have translated into their everyday lives by the sharp division they like to make between fighters and thinkers, games-playing idiots and thin intellectuals. Too often a woman of vitality and intelligence must choose between a soldier-gentleman and Chaucer's clerk.[15] Should she choose the former, she takes a plunge into the past. This man exults in murder, whether of animals or of his fellow-creatures; deep down within him he is still convinced that women are divided into good and bad – and both require the handling of a master. His wife must beware how she responds to his advances: she may be thought forward or impure. Decency must above all things be preserved. Though games and the classics may have taught the English gentleman the beauty of paganism and the joy of the naked body where man is concerned, he is still stuffy in his approach to sex. He rarely brings the freshness of the morning and the joy of the open skies to the love of mistress or of wife. Plush, gilt and silk stockings express the one; pipe, the armchair at the fireside, dinner, and a coldly furnished bedroom, the other. Conversation is a masculine monologue, punctuated by assent. He will be good to his children, provided they are not odd, and will protect his wife. He will never lift her to rapture. She fears, and will probably deceive him.

The intellectual – perhaps by reason of the monastic tradition of learning, perhaps because he finds Jason so revolting – does all that he can to forget the needs of the body. Woman counts as one of them. She is a burden, a responsibility, a distraction, an incursion of the material into a world of contemplation. As for children and domestic life, they would make an end to all thought, to all art. An instinctive life – so he thinks – is possible only in spasms, if at all, for a man with serious mental work to accomplish. If woman persists in keeping him company, then she must shoulder the burdens, tend him and care for him, and leave him alone when he doesn't want her. It is this contempt for the natural play of instinct which eats the heart out of life for many intellectuals, men and women, of to-day. They dread the gift of themselves, the loss of independence which passion would bring, and therefore they never give freely. In part, they are cherishing the medieval tradition that to be worthy of spiritual or mental labour man and woman must go aside and renounce; in part, they are inspired by a tight conception of materialism, in which individuals are hurled like lumps of matter by dynamic forces through space, unable to do more than come near, but never mingle one with another. This view of life and the medieval are combining to destroy our world in lovelessness and despair.

The old-fashioned mind clings to spiritual duties and consolations and the framework of Church discipline as a bulwark against personal licence; the more modern mind is dominated by mechanism – which is, after all, no more than the rational control of matter – and seeks in an intelligent organization of the State, a framework within which each individual is to perform the duties for which he is best fitted. To neither conception is love between individuals, or sex-love between man and woman, important. In effect, personal relationships do not matter. The Christian doctrine of all-embracing love was once potent, but fails to-day because of the foundation of God, dogma, and Church on which it is built and which modern people cannot accept. 'To love thy neighbour as thyself' is also inadequate without knowledge and understanding. But the rational materialists' attitude – such, for instance, is that of the Bolsheviks – to human relationships, in particular to women and sex, is as lacking in the sense of human dignity as the Christian. Monogamy and undiscriminating licence rest upon a common basis of contempt for love and personality, both asserting that the desire of a man is for a woman, of a woman for a man, but no matter whom. Dualism, as ever, is the culprit. Sex-love is to be no more than a physical need – no part of the serious business of life. Science has brought a more modern attitude to matter, which by its effect upon the imagination may change our conception of personality and sex. Force, struggle, solidity, contact, may yield to gentleness, non-resistance, intermingling and uniting – not by an ethical change, but by a change in scientific thought. We shall no longer think of mind and matter as wronging or thwarting one another, because they are not different forces; and we shall no longer be able to separate physical from mental virtue or depravity. We shall no longer value a love that suppresses or disregards the union of personality.

Taboos and superstitions, struggling dynamic individuals or States – how may we set up a new vision? Perhaps what I have written above seems far-fetched to the reader, but I do not think our life can be cut up into compartments. Philosophy and sex are more important in politics than General Elections. The revolt against the all-powerful Christian State began in the assertion of certain people that their love of good fruit and wine or their enjoyment of sex were not worthy of hell-fire. On personal conduct, on our standards of personal relationship, man to woman, parents to children, are built the customs and laws of States and ultimately their national and international policy. It is here, then, with man and woman, that we must begin. I have in mind, as I write, a piece of Chinese porcelain, on which the sage or poet sits with his book and long pipe; a lovely and elegant lady peeps over his shoulder, and close at hand plays an impish child. I do not think that the Chinese who conceived it expected that poet to write bad verses, or, if a sage, to compose worthless philosophy. On the contrary, to love with devotion, to be learned, to have children, are ideas which have shaped the harmony of Chinese life. As compared with their generous acceptance of instinct our Christian dread of sex and horror of the body are obscene.

If we are to make peace between man and woman, and by their unity and partnership change the ideas that govern our politics and our outlook on the world, it is essential that men should make a more determined attempt to understand what feminists are seeking. It is useless to go on abusing, or pretending that this is a matter of minor importance. It is essential also that women should think clearly and continue in courage and honesty of word and action, neither abandoning all for the pursuit of pleasure nor glorying in opportunities for an oppressive morality belonging to past ages. First and foremost, man or woman, we are human beings. There is a great deal of the work in the community which we can each do with equal ability, given equal training and opportunity. There are other tasks which we must agree to delegate to one another, and neither despise the other for performing them. Life and harmony, generosity and peace are the ideals which the best thought of feminism has set before us. We believe that States and individuals can put them into practice. Will man not pause to understand before he continues on the path of destruction and strife, cupidity and war? Can we not persuade Jason from barbarity and Admetus to the abandonment of his fears? To live with vigour, body and mind and imagination, without fear or shame or dread of death; to drive these baser passions from the hold they have upon our morality and our politics – this is what we ask of modern men and women. They can come to it only in a reckless love of one another, a passion that gives again and again without fear of hurt or exhaustion. It is not an abandonment to nature and to instinct that we need. Pure and barbaric instinct is no more. Our bodies are too much impregnated by inherited habit and knowledge, too much surrounded in their growth by the findings of science. Men and women are not creatures of clay, nor disembodied spirits; but things of fire intertwining in understanding, torrents leaping to join in a cascade of mutual ecstasy. There is nothing in life to compare with this uniting of minds and bodies in men and women who have laid aside hostility and fear and seek in love the fullest understanding of themselves and of the universe. You cannot measure it in inches, nor turn it on and off like a tap. You cannot stay it now and indulge it another time. You cannot come to it by religion or by unaided reason, or by the brute courage of sheer physical vitality. Jealousy is death. Dualism is nonsense, compartments unavailing. You must have in you the thought that is creation; life's spring, and the daring of its unconquered waters – so may you transform the world and people it with gods who know no more the hates and littleness of men.

NOTES

1 Lovat Fraser in a cunning article in *The Sunday Pictorial*, January 4th, 1925.

2 An ingenious method of accomplishing this suggests itself. Since women do not sit in the House of Lords, suppose that all Peers' wives, following the example of the Duchess of Atholl, stand for Parliament where their husbands have estates. This would obviate the necessity, now felt by Conservatives, of restoring the veto of the House of Lords.

3 Sir Arbuthnot Lane, for whom I have hitherto entertained an entirely unqualified admiration, in a recent article. *Vide The Weekly Dispatch*, December 28th, 1924.

4 Mumbo-Jumbo was an idol set up by the men in Nigeria to terrify erring women. The men, but not the women, knew him to be a fake. See *Mungo Park's Travels*.

5 There may be a biological cause of the alleged smallness of feminine appetite. Watching a raven and his consort with fresh meat, I observed that she obtained only a minute portion beneath the contempt of the male. Can it be that, in the savage state, only those females survived who could exist on the little the male allowed them? Is this a case of sex-linked heredity?

6 This scheme no longer works, as is evidenced by the attitude of the National Union of Women Teachers this year (1925). Intelligent women are more appreciated than they were, and teachers know they may all want to marry some day.

7 The anti-feminists who see in emancipated women nothing but persecuting spinsters should take comfort from the fact that voluntary motherhood will ultimately destroy feminism, if they are right. The children of women passionately desirous of maternity will inherit strong parental and survival instincts, the occasional feminist 'sport' not reproducing herself!

8 See the service for the *Churching of Women* in the Prayer Book.

9 *Leviticus*, xii, 1–8.

10 An instance of the incredible snobbery surrounding this question is given by the decision of the conference of Headmasters of Secondary Schools, January, 1925, against free secondary education. While the middle-class parent groans against the cost of his children's education, he also refuses to take the obvious remedy of making education free, for fear the working class should get some of it. Class difficulties would not exist if health and education were adequately dealt with.

11 A woman of 45 years of age gave birth recently at Queen Charlotte's Hospital, Paddington, to her 23rd child. Ten children is not uncommon.

12 Professor MacBride, dealing recently with the 'Inheritance of Defect' (*Daily Telegraph*, January 8th, 1925) said: 'The question of questions was whether the failure of the lowest strata of society was due to their surroundings or to their inborn characters. Such questions must be ultimately decided by experiment; and proper experimental work could only be done with animals; we were not entitled to make *corpora vilia* of our fellow human beings. For this reason he would direct attention to the common goldfish, whose weird monstrosities were all originally due to the starvation of the eggs with respect to light and air in the earliest stages of development. The result of this starvation was to weaken the developmental power and to produce a disharmonious arrest of growth of various organs. Similar arrests of growth occurred in human beings, and were the causes of mental and bodily defects. Their original cause, however, must be sought in the starvation and poisoning of the blood of the mother, but, once started, they were hereditary.'

13 Working people live on tinned milk, margarine, and substitute eggs – all deficient in necessary vitamins.

14 I am strongly of opinion that experience of maternity, even more than of marriage alone, would help the teacher. Some women, even teachers, are bored by children until they have one of their own, whereupon all children of all ages become interesting.

15   A clerk ther was of Oxenford also
       That unto logyk hadde longe y-go.
       As leene was his hors as is a rake,
       And he was nat right fat, I undertake,

      .   .   .   .

       And him was lever have at his beddes heed
       Twenty bokes clad in black or reed.

Part Two

THE RIGHT TO BE HAPPY

1927

During the 1920s Dora Russell became convinced that it was foolish and futile to expect that human problems could or would be solved by the invention of bigger and better machines. Only men, she argued, could have thought it sensible to place their faith in the technical products of their prized intellect and to ignore the richness of human resources: only men, she argued, could have constructed a cult of machine worship and expected their god to deliver prosperity and happiness to all.

She wanted to write a book about the machine age and even had a contract for her book (*The Religion of the Machine Age*, published – eventually – in 1983 by Routledge & Kegan Paul), but Bertrand Russell himself was among those who failed to understand what it was that she was questioning, and so she abandoned the project and as a 'substitute' wrote *The Right To Be Happy*. The source of happiness she suggested is really quite simple, so simple that it has frequently been overlooked: it lies within human beings themselves. And her book is an illuminating discussion of the resources which human beings possess – resources of nurturing, affection, intellectuality, creativity, consciousness – and the marvel of being able to reproduce; in a male-dominated society these resources have been devastatingly undervalued but they can be reclaimed and utilised for the good of the individual and society. Our world would be very different, she argued, if the emotions and feelings of human beings were made the basis of our social organisation: there could be happiness and prosperity for all, although the meanings of these terms would also be changed.

The Preface, reprinted here, summarises Dora Russell's case, and the chapter 'The Rights of Human Beings: Food; Work; Knowledge' provides some indication of her examples and her persuasive writing style.

PREFACE

This book attempts two things: first to demonstrate that happiness for all human beings is not only feasible, but the most satisfactory basis for social construction; second to bring to the help of such construction modern theories of the nature of man and the universe. At a time when there is so wide-spread a struggle against national, class, and sexual oppression, it seems important to examine the various claims which are advanced, and to see whether, after all, there is not behind them a consistent new philosophy.

To me at least it appears that people of our time are expressing new ethics and metaphysics against which the old ones may be weighed and found wanting. Such views, however, lie scattered among specialists in the various sciences, in education, and psychology, or are confusedly shouted as slogans of party or sex. We suffer very much in England and America from the rigid separation of thought in the various departments of life. In Russia an attempt at a constructive modern synthesis has been made, and – though this will be displeasing both to the reactionary and revolutionary American – it seems to me that metaphysics and psychology in America are building an intellectual, though not as yet a political, synthesis that is almost identical with that of Soviet Russia. I call this the mechanical synthesis. Newton and Descartes laid the foundations of its metaphysic and Professor Watson has given the latest and most revolutionary expression to its psychology. This synthesis is useful in that it affords hypotheses helpful to scientific discovery; it is harmful when it is accepted as a dogma. As such it does seem to be too frequently accepted, and to be superseding the old medieval sanctions – to which on the

whole it is preferable. But dogmas based on mechanics will
not solve all human problems or successfully promote human
happiness. It is significant that both Professor Watson and
the Bolsheviks are united in their hearty contempt for
heredity and biological sanctions. They are somewhat remote
from agriculture and they like to think that men and human
society can be re-made like a machine to suit a definite plan
in their minds. Professor Watson allows the merest germ of
inborn instinct or nature: the rest of the human creature he
holds to be manufactured by the 'conditioning of his reactions'. The *criteria* by which he – or the Bolsheviks – would
judge completed individuals are reminiscent of industrial
organization: efficiency in action and quantity in output.
Professor Watson, for whose work I have in many respects the
profoundest admiration, comes, in the final chapter of
Behaviourism, to some curious conclusions, which, however,
flow quite logically from his general thesis. He measures the
value of a writer by the amount he is paid per word; in
business he has the typical hustler's outlook; and the value of
a picture seems to depend in his opinion on the number of
people who admire it.

Far be it from me or anyone in this tortured age to
suggest that it would not be well to re-create society. The
world as we know it is a hideous nightmare. Human beings
have made it, and therefore human beings need to be
changed. The chemistry of the human body and the study of
human reactions can give us the means of going beyond
changes of environment to changes in the nature of the
human creature himself. I quarrel merely with the idea of a
plan, according to which all men are at once to be made anew.
The medievalists had such a plan. We were born in sin, and
re-born into the Kingdom of Heaven, with the result that it
became intolerable to us to go on living upon the earth. It has
taken us centuries of thought and mockery to shake the
medieval system; thought and mockery here and now are
required to prevent the mechanists from building another.
Without falling into a mystical vitalism that reverences
organic nature as sacred, we can at least try rather to serve
than to subdue the prancing seas of life. With this in view I
have taken as impulses, instincts, or needs, certain driving

forces in the human species as we know it at present, and argued for such social and economic changes as will give them new, free, and varied expression. To take even this first step towards a happy society is a herculean task. After it has been accomplished generations to come will see what the creature will do next. We none of us know; and we should be thoroughly on our guard against all those who pretend that they do.

DORA RUSSELL.

Carn Voel

Porthcurno, Cornwall

Chapter III

THE RIGHTS OF HUMAN BEINGS: FOOD; WORK; KNOWLEDGE

The foregoing chapters have perhaps convinced the reader that there have existed in the world a great many theories of conduct and a great deal of confusion as to the ultimate ends of life. It will not be an easy task to make all these people happy. Some of them, of course, want to be unhappy, and therefore we shall be doing our neighbourly duty by them if by word and action we help them to that end. I do not suggest active persecution of such people, the shocking spectacle of the happiness of others will suffice.

There seem, also, to be a dozen definitions of this human being whose happiness we so ardently desire. Are we to aim at the happiness of the Cave Man, or the Greek or the Christian, the gentleman, the plutocrat, or the son of toil? Whose definition and morality shall we adopt?

Since I believe in the value of scientific knowledge, I will try to take a simple definition applicable to all, though, of course, they will all refuse to accept it. A human being is a certain kind of conglomeration of processes and chemical reactions which in relation to stimuli and environment produce certain instincts and desires. Of these desires the most peremptory are the need of food and drink, next the needs of activity, sex and parenthood. The last two are distinct and not to be confounded in one impulse. Specifically human is the power of acquiring very complex habits and that form of the instinct of curiosity which, when it acquires knowledge, stores it and hands it on from father to son. Therefore, in the human being we are dealing with a creature whose purely animal reactions are conditioned by a considerable amount of knowledge and technique that have been either almost imperceptibly acquired from the parents or the communal stock of learning, or deliberately learnt by the particular human being himself. This definition of the human being will be decried by the orthodox Christian or moralist as one which takes a low view of humanity, since it derives all from the material and has not due regard for the corruption of sin and the necessary striving upward towards pure spirituality. But as we have already seen, in the light of modern physics and psychology, the mind and matter division is obsolete and nonsensical. The so-called lower impulses are not sin, nor need this agonized battle between human nature and the pagan animal world continue on its old religious and mystical basis. The preying of the animal species one upon another is not wicked, but conditioned by the necessities of their lives. Among all species human beings have displayed the greatest adaptability, variety, and ingenuity and may legitimately claim to be in command of the world. Their instincts for murder and destruction are relics of past struggles – no more. What we have to make plain to modern people is that the advances of knowledge and the possibility of security enjoin on us an ethic of positive creation rather than the old-fashioned, negative struggle for existence with its correlatives in fear moralities and religions. This ethic demands nothing less than the unity of the human race. In laying down the basis of the State, therefore, we must not be bound by old moralities, but attempt a more scientific and impartial attitude which will leave new moralities free to develop and display their worth. We are dealing with a chaotic world in which notions picked up at random have produced an infinite variety of human types, people of muddled thoughts, confused and thwarted impulses, badly bred, badly handled, badly taught from early youth. This is a source of great inconvenience to the legislator who must – does, in fact – often wish that he could once more arbitrarily impose the Christian synthesis.

Other modern legislators, such as the Bolsheviks, try to impose a new synthesis regardless of the traditions and habits of the majority of the human beings that they govern. Even their revolutionary theory of civilization, we may note, is out of date by a couple of hundred years. Apart from the propagandist bias of its schools, it teaches a dogmatic materialistic determinism that derives from the eighteenth century, has not grasped the significance of evolution and biology, nor of modern theories of matter and psychology. The same may be said of America which is a pure eighteenth century State, whose God is the First Cause and whose religion is based on the argument from design as advanced by eighteenth century preachers. These divines were always concerned to show how the natural laws discovered by science displayed and glorified the wisdom and ingenuity of the Creator. The prosecution of Evolution in America is perfectly logical, for the bulk of its people have never grasped it. Their view of science goes no further than medicine, motor-cars, and mechanical warfare. That science can say anything about human character is to them a new and horrible notion. The voice of hundred per cent America spoke through the lady who said to Freud: 'In Austria you may dream those selfish dreams, but in America even in our dreams we are unselfish.'

We must remember, then, in all considerations of individual rights that we are dealing with very great differences in environment and acquired habit, and therefore very different impulses and desires. A community of people who have lived a hundred years with industrialism differs greatly from a race of peasants who for the first time set eyes upon a motor-car. So every human being is compounded of parentage, traditions, environment, and education. It follows that the deliberate creation of certain types of human beings is not an impossible task and one which I shall consider later. At present it is sufficient to say that such a task cannot be undertaken in a revolutionary and iconoclastic spirit. We must beware of State imposition of religious syntheses, even new ones, and concern ourselves with defining the elementary rights of every type of human being. Evolutionary processes are slow, and there never will be an age in which all the citizens are so enlightened as to bear no marks of the superstitions of past times. It is vital, therefore, to conceive of a State which legislates impartially for all, is not to be seized by a few of one type as a mechanism of oppression, and will never persecute minorities or individuals unless there is overwhelming evidence for that course. This last proviso is necessary, for we cannot permit those whose ethics enjoin wholesale murder to indulge their impulses – and this should apply to nations and classes as well as to individuals. Nor can we permit in a community where all have an ample share of what is necessary for life that men and women should rob one another of private possessions. Our laws must involve a certain check on the outworn instincts of greed and fear, and their derivatives hatred and destruction. They can only do this if they and our economic and social system provide the security and liberty which alone render those impulses useless. It is obvious that education will be needed to supplement legislation, for it is not possible in one moment to make life secure for everybody. But from security in small groups we can pass on to larger groups and so ultimately to all human society, provided each group in its turn will do its part towards the eradication of fears. At present within our own society people holding one set of beliefs dread and try to oppress people who hold others. Thus the employer tries to starve men whose opinions he fears; Roman Catholics would like to imprison birth-controllers; Christians try to suppress free thought or free love; militarists torture pacifists: and quite recently men tortured women who aspired to political freedom. This all happens because we have not the right conception of State activity and of the rights of individuals. We live under worn-out laws and customs belonging to the Christian synthesis and manipulated by the possessors of wealth.

The first and most elementary principle of a society that wants to make people happy is to satisfy the primary instincts of human beings. It sounds very simple, but our own society completely fails to accomplish this simple object. The first need by our definition was food: millions of our people do not get enough to eat. 'Life, liberty and the pursuit of happiness' were to be individual rights under the American Constitution, yet in America also people are starving. And the right to life, or food, is not merely a quantitative question.[1] We have not merely to give enough of just any kind of food, but the food must be pure, well adjusted to our needs, nourishing and well prepared. What would be said of a chemist who maintained that he could make a chemical compound with just any quantity of the particular substances he was to combine? What if, not content with that, he were to add that the spirit or soul of hydrochloric acid or whatever it was, was so magnificent that it could rise superior to defects in its chemical composition? Yet this is the sort of nonsense we talk when we are dealing with human mechanism. Fortunately, hydrochloric acid is class-conscious, and takes exactly what it needs to sustain its composition. Nor does it take more. Quantitatively food is important because men, women, and children are starving. Qualitatively food is important, first, because the eating of wholesome well-prepared food is one of the rights and joys of civilized human beings, and second, because by right feeding we can maintain the highest of our present standards of human health and vigour and probably improve upon it, thus adding to the delight of life by greater grace, suppleness and beauty of human bodies. Before the reader turns in annoyance from the childish simplicity of these sentences, will he or she reflect on the changes of government and economic organization that will be required to make them come true. The elementary right to life is explicitly denied in our society by those who make international trade competition the basis of wages. As a state, as individuals they say, we have no right to happiness, we must struggle with others for our existence. The right to life is also denied by those who pretend to affirm it when they attack the limitation of families. They demand that human beings be born though their parents may not have the wherewithal to maintain the structure of a growing human body. They do this on the ground advanced by our hypothetical chemist, that the soul rises superior to material circumstance. Besides the souls of dead babies, if duly baptised by the right brand of magic, will go to a better world. If they die before the magic is applied, or the magic is wrong, they will roast for ever to please a beneficent Deity.

Even supposing society admits the right to life, for there are signs that the public conscience is awakening, we have then the vast problem of reorganizing our food supply. We must procure enough milk or other wholesome food for all the young children and good food for all adults, not only a privileged few. We must regulate producing, buying, importing, packing, and preserving. The farmers, the meat trusts, the millers, the bakers, the cooks and restaurant proprietors must be taught to listen to food specialists, doctors, and mothers. Mothers themselves will need teaching: and cooking, not necessarily done by mothers, will become an important art and science. Think of the problem of persuading the typical old-fashioned feminine woman that both in the home and restaurants she runs – (for there are now many such enterprises run by women) scientific attention to balanced meals must replace snacks, stewed up and overcooked rubbish, tinned foods, and cheap dried preparations. At present, even well-to-do women are far too much inclined to accept as food all that they buy at the grocers and to give it regardless of consequences to themselves and their family.

Health reports from New York on children in their teens who did not come from poverty-stricken families showed that an alarming proportion of these young people suffered from defects which began with digestive troubles due to wrong feeding in childhood. Other defects also could have been remedied but were left to become chronic and difficult of cure. The parents were either ignorant, or careless, or the food supply was being run in the interests of profit and not in the interests of human life. A dull and utilitarian idea of the basis of society? Perhaps, but I doubt if anyone who has tended young children will say so. In this matter of food, those who conduct the State are *in loco parentis* to the citizens, and it is their bounden duty to see that not one of them lacks what is necessary to his health and growth. Nobody should vote for any politician who has not a well-considered scientific policy on a pure and plentiful food supply, its relation to trade and the numbers of the population. Put the present parliament an examination test. I wonder how many would get through? Minds that soar in the regions of bomb-dropping, the 'glories of our blood and state', our brethren in the far-flung British Empire, must not be tethered down to boric acid in the butter or boron in the bread.[2] The cynic will say that we needs must conquer to maintain our food supply. Such cynicism is merely a cloak for incompetence. To take by armed conquest is spasmodic and temporary, the conquest of public opinion alone is enduring. A sound food policy spells peace, birth-control, an eye to the developing needs of other peoples besides ourselves, international control of food-growing and raw materials. Bring in the whole world, not a group or a federation, especially not only the British Empire. On no other basis can the primary right of the human body to food be secure even in the most powerful of modern communities. I do not believe that I speak here the language of Utopia, for everywhere in individuals and classes all over the world, the belief in the right to life is stirring. Year by year, in the teeth of the short-sighted economy preachers, we add to the functions of the Health and Education Departments[3]; and the fall of infant mortality and improvements of public health are evidence of a passionate belief patiently applied by large numbers of people to the conquest of death, suffering, and disease. The most powerful weapon in the hands of the locked-out wage-earner is the dawning belief of mankind in the right to life. We do not suffer like Christians, we mobilize our forces to the attack. The employer is but a symbol of the enemy, a cypher in the history of what we are accomplishing: we are moving forward to the conquest of all that once we feared, and deified it because we feared it. Let our thoughts and words have the courage which our actions already proclaim.

But the conventional moralist will protest, what about excesses of eating and drinking and the necessary balance to be preserved in this respect if we are to be happy. Here again, I think we are dealing with a problem that will ultimately prove illusory. In the first place, it is idle to base our whole morality on the probability of excess, when only a small minority of the people are in a position to attain it. Their number would be less at first in a more equal society. Secondly, excess in almost every instinctive activity is the direct result of previous prohibition or starvation. The very intensity of our hunger (treated by the religious as a deadly sin) is simply derived from the difficulty of the animal in obtaining food. Most of us find from experience that those that over-eat are people in whom there still lingers the fear of starvation. A generation or two of adequately fed ancestors leading secure lives is a better safeguard against greed than negative teaching. Those who fear most are most prone to hate and destroy. Those who have newly acquired wealth are most prone to over-display. The psychological arguments against prohibition of alcohol are the ones most worth consideration. Nations which have cheap alcohol and people to whom wine or beer is a customary drink, acquire in time a natural immunity to excess. I do not mean that drunkenness does not harm them, but that they are but little tempted to drunkenness. Sudden prohibition is a stimulus to instinct which, baulked of that particular form of savagery, will find another that is perhaps more harmful. Drink is not wicked in itself, merely its excesses destroy the body and bring harm to other human beings. The right course would be not to prohibit but to provide and encourage other pleasures and to assist education by making drink not too cheap or easy of access. I would pursue this course with all pleasures that are quite definitely harmful by expert, scientific standards. New and dangerous pleasures of this type – such as drug-taking to Western peoples – I would attempt to exclude, as we attempt to exclude such terrible diseases as bubonic plague. But if an individual were resolutely set on self-destruction by any of these means, we could do no more than isolate him from those to whom he might bring harm and count him lost to the community like the criminal and the insane. Let me make it quite clear that I think it part of the legitimate pleasure of men and women, especially the young, to drink and dance to intoxication from time to time. We should neither deliver them from evil nor lead them into temptation. But the education, daily life and work of all human beings should be such as to render this no more than a recreation like games and certain forms of sport. Neither drinking, dancing, nor sport would be the central pleasure of life to those who had minds and instincts fully developed and freedom for their exercise. One word as to other pleasures that may bring bodily harm. Dangers and risks voluntarily undertaken in sport or games should not be discouraged. They involve a strengthening not a sapping of will and vitality. It is a mistake to imagine that feebleness and passivity are the qualities required to preserve an ideal state. Obviously sport must not minister to cruelty, but in the developing society we are imagining those forms of sport which do so would gradually lose their interest, and die out.

The human instinct for activity has produced all the work which has built up civilization just as the instinct of curiosity has discovered and shown how to utilize all the knowledge on which civilization is based. Both instincts have been exercised to the pleasure and delight of man in opposition to the teachings of religion. Work was laid upon Adam for a curse because he and Eve aspired to knowledge. Both of them could have remained in the bounteous idleness and ignorance of Paradise. It is sound and logical for a religious society to regard as inferiors or as rebels those who minister to its comforts by work or by knowledge. Christians living within the community I am attempting to describe would be at liberty to continue in that opinion, always provided they took their share in the curse of Adam by contributing work for communal needs.[4] We need not ask them to risk mortal sin by contributing to our stock of knowledge, for the contribution might not be worth their damnation.

It is only quite recently that people have realized that a great many men and women work, as children run and play, from a sheer love of activity, and that they do not cease to work when their immediate individual or family needs are satisfied. Piece by piece we uncover the fundamental instinctive life of human organisms that our false standards have overlaid, as a beautiful fresco is uncovered from the whitewashings of the Puritans. I am not trying to say that all work in the doing of it is a pleasure, or that the more work we do the more we like it. Clearly, the majority of mankind are overworked, and their work is monotonous. Therefore fatigue produces the natural reaction of disgust. Yet how many people, even those engaged in hard and dull work, would avail themselves of the opportunity never to do a stroke of work again? Even those who escaped from uncongenial work would speedily get busy on something else. And how many men and women in England at the present time are suffering from a sense of degradation and despair because they are unemployed, not wanted, having no part in the communal life of labour for human needs? This, although unemployment pay and the help of relations may maintain them at a standard of life not much below that to which they have been accustomed? True, in the normal course of things, the State exacts work from the citizen, for without work a community cannot be maintained, but this is far less of an external discipline in our society than most people imagine. Many people enjoy dull work done in fellowship with others, a great number recognize even routine or mechanical work as an essential service and therefore it gives them pleasure. To others work in itself is a pleasure and even a privilege.

Simpler than that is the labourer's love of the soil and the crops, or the mechanic's proud devotion to a machine. Remove the shadow of starvation and overwork and the grudge against an employer and these pleasures would be increased. Every healthy child will toil and construct with remarkable patience and concentration for the sheer delight of activity and the pleasure of running to his parent at last for approval of the creation of his brain and hands. This could be our attitude to the work of adults. Public opinion should encourage creative pride in all forms of activity that minister to life or to the improvement of life's quality. We should judge men and women by what they create rather than by what they possess or destroy. This is again an ethical principle which is stirring and spreading. Those who produce food, coal, machines, those who run mechanism, those who discover science, artists, designers, teachers, mothers, doctors are increasingly conscious that the joy of their work lies in the creative impulses which it exercises. Even those whose work cannot give this sense of creation, can, if it is useful, feel they have a part in communal creativeness. With short hours of labour they would find in leisure a means to express and employ their individual instinct of activity and creation. Thus the city worker delights in his garden, and the manual worker, if not too tired, would take pleasure in books or in art.

Creative activity in this sense is not, I think, widely felt and communally interpreted by more primitive peoples. It is in Western Europeans the product of settled agricultural and industrial habits of life combined with the increase of knowledge and education which have made industrialism possible.

The instincts of activity and of curiosity, work, and

knowledge have become in us closely interwoven. From the moment scientific discovery touched on the work problem, work lost some of its quality of a curse and achieved dignity. In eighteenth century England, intelligence applied itself to agriculture. Afterwards it was busy with industrialism. Probably at bottom it is the application of science to work and physical needs which has been the means of destroying the antagonism between mind and matter. As knowledge progresses, so work becomes more skilled and needs more knowledge and the activities involved in knowledge and work are seen to be inseparably allied. I think this is an important truth too little understood by educators, politicians, and religious people. Properly understood it would wipe out the distinction between the black-coated and manual worker and settle the whole vexed question about higher education not fitting human beings for manual work. Apart from the fact that an increase of knowledge brings to every human being a new stock of interests and pleasures, it also fits him better for doing the most elementary tasks with skill and patience. It will not detract from his physical strength if bodily health receives its right place in his training.

The exercise of the instinct of curiosity is an elementary right of every human being, man, woman, and child, and every individual should be given all the knowledge he or she is capable of assimilating. We must feed the imagination and the intellect as we feed the other organs of the human structure. Boredom and repression, in other words inactivity and atrophy, are the worst enemies of individual happiness. As a climbing plant expands, it seeks hooks and supports on which to use its tendrils. If it cannot find these, the tendrils wave helplessly and the plant flaps about in an inclement wind, a miserable and thwarted being. By the old theories of Christian education, that plant should be humble and not wish to see the world, but rather creep the earth and endure buffeting meekly. Fortunately our ideals of education are fast changing, but we are still less civilized in education than in gardening. Careless about food, the State has been a parent where teaching is concerned, and a parent of the old-fashioned type. There is in our people a great mass of superstitious ignorance, and of carefully taught humility, fear, and repressive virtue. These stand in the way of their own happiness, and the happiness of others. We all know the typical virtuous and self-sacrificing human being who can enjoy no sensible pleasure because he feels it somehow not right; who will sacrifice and work for others, neglecting his own mental and bodily joys till he is no more than an empty shell; then will look at you with an air of gentle pity and long-suffering if you offer him a pleasure. There are more women like this than men because they are more repressed. Inwardly, such virtuous people seethe with envy of those who enjoy what they are incapable of grasping, and with a grudge against those for whom they sacrifice that no amount of gratitude and affection can dispel.

Love for our fellow-men would not have this quality of agonized repression if we ceased to feel that to be virtuous in giving to others we must take away from ourselves. That is not true. Self-sacrifice in danger and devotion in daily work may be glorious, but only when they are inspired by the feeling that we give to create life and joy, not as a sacrifice to a death's-head skeleton of empty virtue. It is a curious paradox that a man whose life is filled with joy will lay it down more cheerfully than one who has led a thwarted and dreary existence. Similarly those who are blessed with every form of happiness, by which I mean not wealth, but sufficient food, exercise for the mind and body, the love of friends, sex-love and children, are those most genuinely anxious to give happiness to others. Saints and visionaries also want others to have the happiness they claim to possess. What we have to do is not to impose our standards upon anybody, but simply to follow our own ideal of happiness for ourselves, seeing to it that we so organize the State that everybody may have the food, work, knowledge and love that are capable of making him happy if he so chooses.

At present there is a vast amount of knowledge which, if taught, would make people happier, more science, more literature, more art; knowledge of bodily processes and sex, and of mental processes in adults and children, better history, more intelligent geography.

I gave the above examples of conduct because I wanted to

make clear that the teaching we give to our citizens is to be of the widest and not coloured by the bias of a particular group, as at present is the case. The Church controls the majority of our schools, especially in rural areas. It would like to re-establish control over all. The Roman Catholics claim the right to censor the advice and teaching given in public welfare centres on the ground that they contribute to the taxes that support them. On this ground, the free-thinking tax-payer might claim to censor the teaching of the Roman Catholic State-aided school. He does so only to demand efficiency in teachers and sanitation in school buildings, but not to dictate doctrine.

On similar grounds to the Catholic plea, the pacifist might dismantle the warships of the State-run Admiralty. We cannot wait for common agreement as to what should be taught, therefore there must be freedom to teach everything and no one must persecute others. Roman Catholics, the Anglo-Catholics, the Mormons, the Buddhists, the Confucians, the Communists, should all be free to teach and parents be free to expose their children to their influence or withdraw them from it. Similarly, free-thinkers and scientists have a right to claim that their children should spend on evolution, psychology, physiology, literature, art, and economics, the energy which they save by not learning religious superstitions. They have a right also to demand a quite different ethical teaching. To this I will return when I speak of the rights of children. But obviously the right to be happy demands that people should in so far as is humanly possible learn what they wish to know, and exercise the talents and faculties which bring them the most pleasure.

We come next to the instinct of sex and the instinct of parenthood, which are distinct, but confused in conventional teaching and thought. These are so important as to require a separate chapter. Here let it suffice to say that there are no instincts less harmful or more productive of delight in the whole range of human instincts and emotions than the desire for sex-love and the desire for children. Neither are completely denied to men in our community, nor to all women, but they are made into burdens instead of supreme joys.

Let us leave then the human being in general with his

right to the joys of life, activity, and knowledge, and turn to consider the happiness and co-operation of human beings in their sexual and parental functions.

NOTES

1 I take food as symbolical of all primary bodily needs, e.g. reasonable warmth, housing, clothes, medical care.

2 Recently the Imperial butter importers protested against the unfair advantage given to Danish butter by purity regulations, and in *The Times*, 28th July, 1925, the Bakers frankly tell the Government that they mean to go on poisoning the public with boron, because the public is ignorant. They say further that they supported the Conservative Government because they expected it to mind its own business, e.g. deal with armaments and not the food supply. Cf. also the recent outcry about arsenic, which had been put into apples, without knowledge or consent of the unfortunate consumers, and the controversy regarding jam, etc., in *The Times*, 20th–22nd September, 1926. Sir Kingsley Wood, speaking for the English Conservative Government, maintains that the housewife should not be encouraged to rely upon State regulation in these respects. Such a position implies that we shall go back to home preserving, hand-mill grinding, and home baking, to which, in fact, many women have already been driven.

3 This was written before the economies of the Conservative Government in England, 1925–6. Public indignation over these economies was great, but powerless against the Conservative majority in the Commons, which is out of all proportion to the number of their supporters in the country.

4 Preaching Christianity is not work by this definition.

Part Three

IN DEFENCE OF CHILDREN

1932

'Children are people too' is a slogan that could have been invented by Dora Russell, who firmly believed that the domination of one human being over another was wrong and unjustifiable, and included children in her definition of human beings. In the face of much sentimental opposition she declared that society did not like children very much and that in the past and the present, and across cultures, the history of the treatment of children was more often than not the history of brutality and cruelty. The first and the last chapters of her book about children's rights have been selected: the first chapter, 'Why Do We Have Them?', for the historical background it provides, and the last, 'The Future', because of the accuracy of her assessment and predictions. Like so many feminists of the last decade, Dora Russell focuses on the oppression that occurs within the home and the family and pleads for new forms of social organisation that are more just, and more liberating. In one of her rare moments of despondency she suggests that unless changes are made, it is possible that, in this industrial age, women will simply stop having children because the strain will be too much, and that the 'magic' of being able to reproduce will decline. Fifty years later, she looks at all the women who have elected not to have children – and wonders.

Chapter I

WHY DO WE HAVE THEM?

Children, so parents of the nineteenth century would have told us, need no defence. Every mother is glad to see them born, every father ready to support his brood, every right-thinking man or woman to see that no harm should happen to a little child. Even the wild beasts of the jungle and the prolific cat will cherish their young against a hostile universe; how, then, should man, the image of his Maker, prompted alike by animal instinct and the diviner side of his nature, stand in need of any admonition to defend the issue of his body? How often have the hearts of respectable men and women, sitting by the fireside, thrilled at the cry 'Women and children first!' as they listened to tales of shipwreck, fire, and the atrocities of the Hun on the Belgian babes; how often has the middle-class mother clicked tongue and knitting-needle over the unnatural proletarian of the temperance fable who does not prefer the children to the drink? How often from the hearth-rug pulpit has *paterfamilias* delivered his moving sermon on the place and whole duty of woman and the secrets of the mother heart? How many million parental eyes streamed tears as the radio told, but recently, of the fate of one American child?

Yet nineteenth century English children turned out to the loom in cold winter dawns, the children of war heroes grow up workless and half-starved, the housing conditions of the poor continue to drive fathers and even mothers to the warmth of the pub parlour; while *paterfamilias* chastises his sons into manhood, charms or bullies his daughters into subservience, calls for strict economy in the social services, is suitably outraged at all this talk of sex and birth control. He makes his pile, keeps firm control of capital and income and finally dies wondering why, after a life of sacrifice, he should be cursed with such a useless and ungrateful family. Amid the cries of shame that our modern world cannot even provide safety for rich men and women to bring up their young without fear of violence, our loving fathers gather round the international conference table whereat, having eaten and drunk well, they talk of dignity and pomp and circumstance, haggling meanwhile over the length of guns, the size of submarines, or an extra half million of paper debt. Our loving mothers join committees for the better enforcement of prohibition, or the closer surveillance of young criminals and wicked aliens, or the propagation of the gospel among the unregenerate coloured peoples. Perhaps the honestly bewildered among them seek forgetfulness in the cocktail party or at the bridge table. They know, of course, that there are a lot of 'cranks' with all kinds of remedies for the terrible world in which we live. But it is all too difficult to follow and anyone who is fool enough to get mixed up in reforms will probably end in gaol or some poor law institution.

It is painfully obvious, when anyone begins to look below the surface, that it is hate rather than parental love that rules the world, and that children are not the first but the last thing our society cares for.

People do not have so many children as they used. But they do go on having them. One wonders why. 'They don't think about the children till afterwards,' said a ten-year old boy to me once, 'or else they just like having someone to boss around.' Prompt and to the point. In past times, certainly, children were born because their parents did not know how to prevent conception. And when one writes 'past times' in that connection, it is necessary to recall that throughout China, India, South America, the greater part of Russia, Spain, Italy, Africa, and amongst the bulk of adults in the so-called civilised countries, ignorance of biological mechanics still remains a prime reason for having large families. In fact, it is not really in past times at all, but in the very present, that parents are forced to make a virtue of necessity and to pretend they love the children who descend upon them – 'afterwards' – as the price of instinctive pleasure. Biologically, indeed, we may be said to 'love' our children, as we love ourselves. They are a part of our own expansion into space and time, our desire as a species to conquer the earth. Men and women want to prevail, to be effective – a man to number with .pride the children who bear his name, a woman to see her own body spill forth and spread its fruit over the earth as the dividing amoeba scatters its progeny. For this reason the literature of rising nations and of growing tribes is full, like the Bible, of concern with fruitfulness, of glory in the seed which is as numerous as the sands of the sea-shore. Short-lived and fragile species, the biologists tell us, multiply rapidly and in great numbers. The offspring quickly mature, reproduce again with speed and die as soon as these functions are fulfilled. More stable animals have a longer period of life and of infancy, and a correspondingly smaller number of descendants. Longer infancy, slower and smaller reproductive powers necessarily force upon the animal greater concern for the fate of the young. Herein is the source of what we call parental love. It is no more than a part of the struggle of the species, a sort of biological imperialism, an offshoot of the struggle for power. In those creatures who develop a psyche, parental love necessarily contains within itself the hate and possessiveness that accompany ambition, even when these are unconscious.

The biological family is concerned, then, only to rear children to an age at which they can fend for themselves. In different species, and for man at different times of his development this age will, of course, vary. The butterfly, its utmost maternal functions rapidly performed, passes a brief and care-free existence; the thistle scatters its down upon the wind and returns promptly to the selfish consolidation of its own forces; the mother stickleback, lured for a brief space into the love nest prepared by the male, lays her eggs and returns with speed to the flowing liberty of the river. Mating love, indeed, in any bisexual species lasts just long enough to ensure fertilisation. Few are the species in which it is not at strain before the infancy period of the young is over. Disillusion waits on him who overestimates the altruism of the creative forces.

War and pestilence and famine, in the familiar doctrine of Malthus, were in the past the checks to the increase of human population. Cave-people, beset by every kind of danger and at first practically without tools or weapons, must have increased very slowly. Maternal concentration on the young needed to be very intent if any were to survive. The nomadic peoples, too, were haunted by the fear of extinction even when they had large flocks and herds and had begun to organise their tribal life. But I should imagine that, as this way of life emerged, the male became more involved with biological construction and less with the mainly destructive pursuits of hunting and fighting. He would be constantly preoccupied with animal fertility in his flocks and herds. He would number them and cherish the cows and ewes at parturition, and be led on to the numbering of his wives and children. In the hardships of such a primitive life the death-rate of mothers and babies must have been very high and the infancy period very brief. Children of lake-dwellers perforce learned to swim at the age of a year or else drowned; at three or four or very little older the girls must have begun to help with the domestic life and the boys to imitate the pursuits of their fathers.

The interests of the family were paramount. Each individual was bound to serve them and to exercise what skill or foresight he had in order to achieve biological survival. In nomadic life, as the family extended to the tribe, there would be a very slight increase of individual liberty, through the increase of occupations. Tent-making, weaving, butter-making begin for women, and the life of shepherd and cow-herd for men. Maternal concentration begins to spread itself over domestic pursuits. Each mother is able to rely to some small extent on the security which the larger group affords in caring for the young. She would have help from other women and from the older girls. In men the sense of property increases proportionately with their growing control of the food supply and the conditions of life. The older men of the tribe take rights in everything, including the women and children; there develops the patriarchal system that the Old Testament describes, in which younger sons must increase the tribe by raising up seed to their older brothers, in which men buy wives by years of service to their fathers, and receive endowment with them by the gift of a proportion of the flock.

Barren wives give slave women to their husbands to increase the family.

On the steppe, under the Soviet jurisdiction, this way of life is to be found nearly in its pristine state. At a very early age, and in all sorts of frightful conditions of winter snow, the children are pressed into the service of the tribal flocks and herds. A recent Soviet film depicts, with moving tragedy, the attempt of a young Communist woman teacher, far out on the steppe, to gather the children into the school-house and educate them. At first she naïvely refuses to concern herself with the bickerings of the tribe over the ownership of sheep. What are economics to her? She has come to teach the children; their lives, for her, are distinct from those of their elders. But she is disillusioned, when on a bitter winter's day the Bey, who claims ownership of the whole tribe and of their labour, enters her schoolroom and by intimidation removes her class one by one that he may put them to work. The little eyes and faces, that had begun to sparkle and glow with the dawning realisation of their individual lives as children and with the vision of a world of knowledge hitherto undreamed of, cloud over and settle into the stolid melancholy of the Mongolian. Cowed and beaten they return to the ancestral slavery. As the story moves to its climax, it is from the younger mothers of the tribe that the organised defence of the children comes.

Human life has moved on, in most parts of the world, from the habits of the nomad to the settled ways of agricultural communities. But children became, in this stage, even less free than before. Not so many of them died when hazards were less, so that they were more of a burden to the parents unless they could be put to use. The larger the family, the stronger and more fruitful the wife or wives, the more vigorous the children, the less might any individual hope for liberty and the greater would be the wealth of the man at the head of all. Russian peasant fathers urge their sons to seek a healthy young wife so that through her and her children there will be many strong hands to till the soil. To this day, on remote farms in Canada or Australia, a family of twenty or twenty-five will obviate the need of employing outside labour. In *Sussex Gorse* Sheila Kaye-Smith has told the story of an English farmer, who bred ruthlessly from a fragile wife that he might have sons to extend his domain by conquering the wasteland surrounding his farm. Their blood, like human sacrifice, is spilled in the process; but corn and pasture rise, where formerly there reigned nothing but tough heather and gnarled furze. The history of negro slavery in Southern America is a blood-stained epic on the same theme. Slave women, slave children, slave men, from dawn to dark, from cradle to grave, spilled out their lives to create wealth for the patriarchal owners. So did the Jews in Egypt create wealth for Pharaoh, so did the teeming families of China enrich the Son of Heaven and his Empire, so do the children of Japan to-day serve their father the Mikado, so all over the world have they toiled in the name of fathers and of kings. The fruit of the womb has been used to conquer the earth; in sweat and death it is given back to the earth from whence it came; power and wealth have come to a species that, as its numbers increased, could more and more afford to be reckless with its young.

What else, many will say, could be expected in the conditions under which human beings have been obliged to live? This is no more than the story of the struggle for existence. True: but the results of that struggle on human law and custom have been far-reaching, the psychological results delicate and profound. All of these are still with us. Our more complex way of life, our greater security, our increased scientific knowledge, these are all very recent in human history. The motives from which we act, in biological matters, lie buried deep in our past.

The struggle for existence was a fact of which every man and woman in primitive times was directly aware. The able-bodied in the prime of life were best fitted to cope with it. While tribes still lived from hand to mouth and in part by warfare, the lives not only of children but of the old men and women were far from secure. Some tribes put to death their leaders as soon as signs of old age began to develop. Sons were needed, just as they are to-day, not only to produce wealth but to defend the tribe against attack, or to prey upon weaker neighbours. Insecurity, it must be remembered, is of two kinds – fear of a failing food supply and fear of violent death.

When men live by hunting, these two are intermingled; in settled agricultural communities they become distinct and then have somewhat different psychological effects. But at each stage the fundamental instinct is similar: losses have to be repaired by the unfailing supply of fresh descendants, whether they be used as the raw material of warfare or as the labour that supplies wealth.

To the strong in the prime of life belonged, in the first instance, every right. He could, and did, kill his elders when they became useless; and, unable to stem the flood of children, he reserved the right to destroy them if they were weak or could not be fed or put to use. A fact of prime importance is that the right to destroy the young persisted long after a morality for preserving the old had been developed. The Greeks and Romans practised infanticide; in modern times the Chinese father sells or kills his children in time of famine. Every increase in property and security put added power into the hands of the old men. They became increasingly concerned and increasingly able to preserve themselves and to prolong their lives at the expense of younger rivals. As their strength began to fail they were swift to perceive the necessity of some law or morality which should protect them when their fighting capacity no longer availed. It was therefore essential for them to control property and to develop taboos that would promote docility in the children. Hence the horror and taboo attaching to murder of father or mother, which is to be found in the Roman law, and the injunction to cherish them laid down in the Mosaic code. There is not a word in the whole Ten Commandments about the rights of children. But there are injunctions as to their duties. God, property and parents are the objects of prime concern. Neighbours' wives, oxen and slaves are to be made secure from theft, but the only compassionate injunction is the preservation of the old. Strange, that the earliest roots of pity should lie in the fears of old men!

Filial piety among the Chinese and the mediaeval and modern Europeans reached an ever greater refinement. The merest shadow of disobedience or disrespect to father or mother brought dishonour upon the offending son. Daughters, under a more threatening shadow of death or punishment, would scarcely entertain a disobedient thought. A correlative of patriarchal power was, of course, patriarchal responsibility. The head of the household might be enriched by his family; he was also in a measure bound to extend them help and protection. He could not, in honour, banish the poor relation from his share of the food at the common table. But that obligation was strictly limited and starvation by disinheritance might be the lot of disobedient sons. Daughters might be sold or given away, or, in mediaeval times, confined to a celibate institution. *A man had a right to do what he liked with his own*. This right, especially as to property, is still upheld by the laws of the majority of countries.

The history of mankind, from the time when there was first any society that could be called civilised, has been a prolonged struggle on the part of the individual to free himself (and then herself) from biological slavery. So soon as there was anyone with leisure to reflect upon human existence, it was seen that the terms on which life could be lived were scarcely to be borne. Sex and food were compelling desires, and yielding to them brought with it submission to all the demands of current tribal morality. There is very little evidence of any conscious desire for children, or of love and delight in them as such, or any sense of the joy of biological creation. Women may have known and felt it, but they were not vocal, and perforce expressed their contributions to life in terms of contributions to the men who owned them. Fertility was held in honour, but more because it was a necessity and a source of pride than because it was a delight. And the first assertion of men and women, as individuals, was to cut themselves off, by asceticism and celibacy, from the common animal fate.

In India, China, in later Greece and Rome, then sweeping across mediaeval Europe, came this movement towards asceticism – a dim feeling that some way must be found by which an individual could possess himself alone. Not to be in bondage to others, or to the tribe, or to the conditions of biological life! By destroying himself, as it were, the ascetic created himself anew, even though he must live in a world of dreams. The refuge of the monastic order was not so much a dedication to God as to oneself, a search for whatever powers might be developed from within. Inside convent walls were quiet and order, deliverance from noise and gasping effort. The vow of chastity relieved a man from incessant family cares and it freed woman from the agony of childbirth and the labours of maternity; the vow of poverty freed both from the burden of property or the urgency of seeking the daily bread. To stifle desire, and thereby escape into a world where imagination alone is king! Before the slavery of poverty and uncertainty, of wealth and comfort, of dependence on man or wife, of responsibility for children – before all these things and their accompanying anguish, the spirit of man was in flight. So soon as the toil of the majority could buy this escape for a few, these few gladly accepted the sacrifice.

It is significant that the very core of the revolt was the refusal of marriage and children.

The influence of asceticism on human society and human relations among Western peoples has been tremendous. Though oriental in origin, it has bitten less deeply into the life of the East. Wealth, for the oriental, is still counted in biological terms. When poor, he is thin, when rich he waxes fat; he has a preference for women who are sleek and rotund. Gold and jewels, silken carpets and hangings, baths, perfumes, spices and delicate foods, many lovely wives and slave girls, abundance of comely children, mules and horses, palaces and gardens – with delight and pleasure the oriental spreads himself in space and time and wards off the thought of toil and death. His power-desire is gratified by immediate personal power over living beings and possessions around him. The plastic arts and poetry please him. But the sciences, born at his elbow, passed into the heritage of the West.

The Westerner, bowing his neck to a religious asceticism, contented himself on the whole with a sparer life, cut down his wives to a (nominal) one, with a consequently smaller family, and set his hopes of happiness in the future rather than in the present. For a long time pent within religious dreams, thwarted of pleasures and consequently savage for power, the Western Europeans lived in actual and psychic conflict, amid bitter ecclesiastical persecutions. Every law and custom of their society bears the marks of that conflict. But perhaps no greater battle in the history of human civilisation was ever fought. For at the end of it Europe emerged, holding aloft the lightning shaft of knowledge – science, the fruit of contemplation, a descendant, at long last, of monkish prayer and fasting, austere, exact and terrible, no longer a dream belonging to the hereafter, but, as it were, God made manifest, a dream that could subdue the inanimate world.

The biological cost has been great, for the instincts of those who derive from the mediaeval tradition have been badly twisted. But, proportionately, the sense of the value of the highly differentiated individual has been a gain upon which the whole of humanity may now build. Through our denial of the family in order that thought might live, we have achieved a position from which every problem of human existence looks different. We can approach our difficulties with hope instead of with fear, with power to control, rather than with makeshift panic, with a sense of creation, rather than with unwilling service to life against overwhelming odds. Those who, by a sacrifice of immediate animal needs, lifted themselves above the battle to think or to prepare for the future have made possible a wider and securer and more intelligent life for all.

It is from this angle, I think, that we must view the Puritan psychology and the painful rise of the industrial system, which was a part of that psychology expressed in economic life. As an end in itself asceticism is barren; the results of its attitude to human feelings are highly dangerous. It dams up love and pleasure to give an exit for human energies in power. And power rather than wealth, or the use of wealth as power, has become the keynote of the modern Western world. But power has been what humanity supremely needed. Now that we have power in our hand, the test of our generation comes. It is we who must use it.

The effects of scientific knowledge and of industrialism on family life have been many and varied. They have produced a wild confusion in which the majority are still groping. The first result, for the children, was that more of them survived and were the victims of a still more merciless exploitation. But two forces came into being to assist parental helplessness and also to curb parental power. These were, first, the growth of a close-knit, relatively secure and prosperous state; and, second, the discovery of birth control.

For the first time the community was seriously able to assume collective responsibility for the non-productive units; the old, the sick, the very poor, the very young. Patriarchal concern for the unfortunate members of the family began to be superseded by state help. It became possible by state control and compulsory education to prolong enormously the period of infancy and of preparation for life. The rich, as a matter of pride and social advantage, had already begun to do this by giving education to their sons and at long last to their daughters. Upper-class education set a man on the road to a dominant position; it made the daughter a more amusing and interesting marriageable commodity. I do not attribute the conferring of these advantages in any great degree to parental affection, since the happiness of the children does not seem, to judge by the manner and type of education given, to have been the prime object.

If this judgment seems hard, let the reader for a moment consider with what tenacity compulsory education for poor children was fought; how only yesterday bitter opposition to the raising of the school-leaving age came from parents of all classes, including the parents of the poor themselves. Nor can one easily forget the passionate battles of the nineteenth century against factory legislation, against the liberation of slaves, or, to-day, the refusal of the English Parliament to reduce the working week of adolescents even to the level of that of adult men and women. No: parental love is weak indeed when it comes to the sacrifice of parental profit or prestige. Parental affection and responsibility, filial piety, the preservation of the sacred family unit – all these are repeatedly urged. The naked cry of thwarted power is ashamed without a dress of sentiment.

But against it all, tenacious (and often celibate) busy-bodies have succeeded in erecting some structure of health and educational services, some legislation for the rights of infants and children and young men and women.

Birth control is the greatest discovery of all; since by it for the first time in human history love is set free. When people are no longer bound to have children they can discover freely whether they really want them. The price of ascetic self-denial need no longer be paid; men and women are able at last to distinguish between their desire for each other and their wish to reproduce themselves. They can think, before instead of 'afterwards', of the pleasure or pain involved in those children they plan to 'boss around'. And they must needs reflect on these matters in a society that has now begun to set bounds to that bossing, will no longer allow unbridled freedom for exploitation, and will even help somewhat with the burden of children. The fall in the birth-rate speaks eloquently of the joy our generation is experiencing in that liberation.

For certain young Europeans just before the war life held out greater possibilities of happiness than perhaps had ever been known before. They could get free of the family in which youth had been spent and, adequately educated by the State to the point of earning a living, could go out to enjoy an individual life in work and in personal relationships. As always, the first taste of liberty was an intoxication. The present was theirs; the future could for the moment be forgotten. Behind them lay the heritage of Puritan effort, a secure and prosperous society whose Puritan morals were decaying, leaving them free for generous enjoyment, rather than bound to mean self-denial and provision for times to come. They looked forward to a period of sex expression, ending probably in a marriage with a small family. Joint earnings would help the economic problem and provide, for the adults, individual achievement to supplement self-projection into the family. Individuals themselves, happy and unfrustrated, except in so far as their upbringing might have harmed them, they prepared to treat their children as individuals from the moment of birth. And here, in my belief, with the laying off of the hand of compulsion, whether upon man and wife or upon parent and child, for the first time the hope of real love was born. For love is *knowledge* of a person; a being on the side of a person; a concern for that person's uniqueness; a refusal to subjugate him (or her), unless by his own willing consent in love, to anyone else's needs but his own.

The growing security of our society, up to the outbreak of

the war, was a growing inducement to men and women to lead self-centred lives. There were many varieties of salaried occupations and work could be found suited to the capacity and intellectual development of the individual. Something could usually be laid by for old age; and when not, a pittance was granted from the State in some countries. Better health and education had begun to make the whole of life more interesting and pleasant and to postpone death by quite a number of years. For women, especially, great changes came towards the end of the nineteenth century. Celibate men and women of past times have, consciously or unconsciously, consoled themselves for the lack of descendants by the hope of personal immortality after death. But only recently the modern man and woman scarcely needed even this consolation if their earthly lives were long, happy and effective. With the threat of death removed to distant old age and a good life in store, young men and women very naturally postponed or avoided the problems of parenthood. Parenthood had, so far, always been a heavy and inescapable burden; few were really conscious of it as definite need. Those who were conscious began to see it, when voluntary, as something fresh and new, a creative art and science worth undertaking, under good conditions, for its own sake. Those who were sensitive among parents and teachers began to realise the true psychological problems of the family. In school and in home the art and science of child-nurture began to be taken seriously. Idealists awoke to a new happiness for parents and teachers and, if this new attitude to children could become widespread, to brilliant hopes of racial and social improvement.

The opposition to the new point of view was, of course, tremendous. It came alike from the tenacious old and from the newly liberated young. Children were enough trouble, anyhow, when reared by the older haphazard methods; why should anyone bother to have them if their special interests were going to demand greater skill, time, and sacrifice? Why especially should the modern young woman, with the whole world opening before her, be summoned back to the cradle and the nursery just because some cranks had announced that children were more interesting and important than had hitherto been thought? Her impulse was to resist blindly what might be merely a new trick of the old to enslave her to maternity. She had reason to distrust the old, who had fought women's emancipation, who still wanted women to suffer without anaesthetics in childbirth, who prevented her access to birth control advice, her economic independence, her rights or endowment as a mother.

And did the State care, except to have healthy warriors against other States? Did the employer care, except to see that the supply of cheap and fairly competent labour was not cut off?

Let someone else have the trouble now, said the newly liberated woman. Wipe out the children, let the race decrease, unless better conditions for the mothers could be found. Woman intended to live the life of a civilised human being.

And yet, against everything, with grim persistence, the biological summons repeated itself, first in the female and then in the male heart. Children, it prompted, are no longer the servants of the past, as you yourself are no longer unless such be your wish. The old need not be your chief concern; you are not bound to serve them. Nor your children to serve you. If you are worth anything, you are their servant. For they, and not you, hold the future and can, with your help, create a different world.

Then, into a world beginning to take for granted the hope of food and comfort for all, fell the disaster of a war made highly destructive through science. Even comfortable well-off people were called upon to die horrible and violent deaths. Everyone's sense of values was heightened; the modern became more modern, the old clung more fanatically to reaction. During the war itself, the clash between the new morality and the old had never been more manifest. The moderns stood by, powerless, or went to martyrdom, while fathers and mothers gave their sons to death, became exalted over the sacrifice, and called for more and better cannon fodder. And while in Europe the rebel generation went down in slaughter or in childless spinsterhood, the younger ones grew up under grandfatherly tutelage, many of them unaware of their parents' dreams, or of what those parents might have accomplished for them. They grew up to a contracting instead of an expanding world, a world of closed avenues and shut gates, of hardship, worklessness and disillusion in the place of prosperity, effort and hope. The better world, that had looked so near at hand, was not going to be achieved without a bitter struggle and the loss of more human generations. Among the weary and the despondent, in Western Europe, the birth-rate fell still lower; among the vigorous and idealist, as in Russia, it rose, or maintained its numbers.

This, then, is where we stand to-day, and the issues are pretty clear. Civilised men and women do not care to go on living unless life seems to them worth the effort. They do not care to breed, now that they need not, unless the world offers something to their children. The food supply is enormously increased since the nineteenth century, as also the mechanism of comfort; in all classes there are people who know that starvation may be forever conquered. The possibility of a more abundant life is so evident that the traditional ways are only accepted sullenly under threat of the bomb and the machine-gun. But though starvation need not threaten, we are conscious since the war and the subsequent era of revolutions that a violent death may lie close at hand. At the same moment, science has given us the means to make children precious by prevention. At long last, children have acquired a scarcity value.

Men and women react in various ways to this situation. The hardy among the comfortable classes tend to increase their families, because they may lose sons and daughters through aviation and war. The sternly brave and idealistic or those who are so biologically tough as to be incurable optimists, dare to put out good or better specimens of themselves into a dangerous world. The sensitive and hesitant in all classes will not fling others into the maelstrom, but severely limit their families or condemn themselves to childlessness. Among these, the heedless and irresponsible take all that society can give them and beguile the boredom of their days in the search for new and amusing sensations, playing innumerable variations on the theme of personality.

While the old, past child-bearing and past learning,

refuse to recognise the need for change; they weep salt tears for their happy past, and crocodile ones over the sad present they have made. Some of them sit in the seats of power and wealth, applying old solutions to new problems and ruthlessly frustrating the effort of the young.

The propertied classes are in the saddle. For them the old ways still run, and the need for change is less apparent. They can still maintain the semblance of the patriarchal system, hoarding money for their chidren, keeping their families from sinking by concentrating the descent of wealth on the eldest son and helping their daughters to make good marriages. They can afford to nurture and educate their children well, and who shall blame them for doing so, as individuals? It is their collective acts which are bad, for though they perfectly realise they are educating their children for a world of social and economic inequality, they are tireless in their efforts to secure its continuance. They will deprive the poorest of anything sooner than sacrifice one jot of what they have themselves. Nor can the majority of them see far enough to realise that there might be spiritual benefits for their children and themselves, if they would come out boldly on the side of change. Spiritual gains, anyway, interest them but little, despite the professions of their religion.

The proletarian parental psychology is different. Their power rights as parents are curtailed. They can derive little profit from their children now, their ability to help them is not great, and they have no property to leave. The power and status of old people in the working-class is the very opposite from that of the wealthy. Without strength or possessions, living under the break-up of family taboos, they can neither control the actions of the young, nor compel the young to take care of the fading creatures who bore them. The proletarian, therefore, has a great deal to gain by an increase in that collective responsibility of society as regards children which is expressed in the social reforms begun during the past century.

Why then do people have children? Because they were and are ignorant of how not to; because children may be a present profit and an insurance against old age; because they will give the parents racial immortality to compensate for individual frustration. Rare indeed is the parent, but becoming less so, who likes his child because he is different from himself.

Shall we ever succeed in transforming the impulse that makes the child a vehicle of the parental ego? One wonders. Listening once to a bedtime conversation between three children of five to six years educated on modern lines, I heard the dilemma purely and logically put.

'Will you marry me, Jane, when we are grown up?' says Billy to a girl of five. 'No, I'm going to marry Jones' (the chauffeur), says Jane. 'But you can't. He will be much too old for you. You must marry me.' 'Then I shall marry Kate,' puts in a second boy called David, uneasy at being left out. But Billy severely reminds him that Kate is already promised to another and, turning to his newly-affianced, he adds, 'When we are married I shall put seed into you and you shall grow babies.' All contemplate that prospect and David continues lonely. 'When we're all dead,' asks David, 'will it be the end of the world?' 'Oh, no,' says Billy. 'Our children will grow up then.' 'When *they* are dead,' persists David, 'will it be the end of the world?' 'Oh, no!' triumphantly from Billy and Jane, secure in the hope of endless progeny, 'it goes on and on and on and on.' Silence, while David reflects sadly on his celibacy. 'I wish,' he ventures at length, 'I could be both a boy and a girl at the same time.' He goes to sleep nursing the hope of reproducing himself bisexually, with no wife at all. But later he confides to a trusted adult the forlorn discovery that 'if you do not marry, *you are dead*'.

It was to escape this death that his parents bred him.

Chapter XI

THE FUTURE

Children, like women and the proletariat, are an oppressed class. A book that sets out in their defence is unavoidably concerned, in the main, with destructive analysis of their oppressors. A constructive policy may be outlined, but is useless without a clear vision of the necessity for destruction and the courage and will to destroy. There are times in history when we can no longer 'broaden down from precedent to precedent' like the English law, and I fear that this is one of them. Everyone feels bewildered and insecure, whether as wage earner or employer, wife or husband, mother or father. Sometimes I think that humanity will prove incapable of the strain of industrial life and large scale organisation; that, after a period of diminishing population and suffering, those left alive will return to agricultural ways of life and the old pattern of the family. We all have divided hearts and in times of strain are fearful of the future. In such moods we take refuge, like the nineteenth century romantics in Europe, in escape into fantasies or study of the past. We have that choice to-day. None of us who are over thirty can really participate in the future; our past binds us. But we can make the future possible or take our stand in the trenches of reaction. We are like a bridge between the old world and the new. Our spars creak and joints break loose; the stress is well-nigh unbearable. When we go down, perhaps continuity will break; the very old will die, and the new world will be free. But it is not quite so simple as that. For the new world is being built out of what we dreamed when we were young. Our dreams must help it still. And if we fall, the old are ready behind us, eager to pass the gulf and catch the young generations in flight. Our task is clear. At all costs the new world must rise beyond us; at all costs the crossing must be defended. We turn to face the envious old. And we must stand, summoning all our peers, like Roland at Roncevaux, to fight the rearguard action in order that the main army may march safely away. Not even in death must we sound the ivory horn to bring them back.

The mediaeval synthesis is dead. It towered above us like a Gothic edifice and generation after generation has chipped at its stones, dragged at its foundations to try and make it fall. Now, as it comes apart we see how grand and complete a structure it was. God, and the King and the Queen and the High Altar, buttressed about by the feudal system and the patriarchal law, held in place by the same pattern implicit in family life, in the law court, the university, the school; authority, in the name of spiritual values, telling us what was right and wrong, demanding the submission of our bodies and our lives. We cut off kings' heads, but kingship could not die so long as we continued to teach the fantasy that made it, so long as we did not relinquish our own royal prerogative within the family. If we want a new society all that symbolism has to go.

The new society demands that women should give up rearing their families in small exclusive homes, treating their children as possessions and as pawns in the game of social rivalry with the neighbours. Women have to give up catching a husband and assuming the right thereafter to dispose as they please of everything within the home that he provides. Men have to give up the idea that all within this home is their personal property, bought and paid for by them, theirs to fling into want or theirs to wrap in the cotton-wool of luxury, whichever their personal ambition dictates. These little fireside kings and queens must abdicate. Power must be expressed by new symbols.

But surely such radicalism is not implied in the simple task of improving the conditions of children? This work can go forward steadily, many will say, within the confines of our present order. The family must remain the basis. It is the keystone of health and social stability. Those who want to tamper with it are merely selfish free lovers, who do not understand the meaning of sacrifice. This is the usual line of reactionary defence. Those who follow it are wilfully blind to the fact that the old family pattern has outlived its uses. It is being attacked, not in the interest of sexually irresponsible cynics, but in the interest of children and social well-being. The family does not do what is claimed for it. Its economic basis is unsound. It is not the best way available of producing and rearing mentally and physically healthy citizens. It is not adequate as a means of making adults and children happy nor of promoting emotional maturity and achievement. Its assumptions have scarcely any common ground with what modern people mean by love and morality. For modern people do mean something by these terms; something that is very real and definite, and far from easy.

It is claimed that our laws, especially in regard to marriage, are directed to the protection of women and children. We saw that, in actual fact, they do not protect children from disease and starvation, and still only to a very limited degree do they secure for them a healthy prolonged infancy and adequate education. Social legislation on matters of health and education is a very recent development. The marriage laws are built on a guilt complex and embody possessive rights in regard to goods and human bodies. In regard to parentage the underlying purpose of the law is to establish the family status and descent of the child. Even here its record is not brilliant. It does not adequately compel either parent to fulfil parental duties, especially as to inheritance. Its procedure towards criminals, especially young ones, is incredibly stupid and brutal. The law, in fact, is looking backwards instead of forwards. It barely touches, and usually hinders, the emotions and morals that are current to-day.

We saw that the State that pretends to uphold a rigid family system is actually already subsidising the members of the family as separate entities. We saw that, however imperfectly as yet, school communities begin to treat children from an early age as individuals without relation to their origins. The schools begin to set them free from their parents' poverty; even, sometimes, from their parents' riches. The school is to some children a refuge from parental unkindness, an escape from parental domination in thought or choice of work. It may be a haven from the dislocation of parental quarrels.

Mothers are seeking liberty to do work of their own and wider choice in loving. When they are not deeply interested in children they would prefer to do their own work. When they love children, they tend to go out and help the children of others by maternity care or by doctoring or teaching, if they are allowed. We may as well be clear as to what all this means. If we were, it could all be freed from class prejudice and the stigma of charity. It means that, more and more, each man and woman is being held to stand in a parental relation, not only to his or her own child, but to every child in the community. No child need be born tainted or defective, no child need starve, or grow up without the chance to be the best possible person in mind and body. We are all responsible, if this occurs. This implies true democracy and a classless society. I see no other road to the goal. The child might become, not in sentiment only but bluntly and practically, the symbol of love.

Has the child been the centre of love in Christian symbolism? Perhaps he was meant to be, but as things stand to-day he certainly is not. Papal encyclicals expressly forbid those very things that the modern holds to be essential to child and adult welfare – the prevention of the birth of unwanted and diseased children, easy divorce or a new basis for marital morality, emancipation of the child from strict parental authority, sex enlightenment of women and children, economic freedom for women, the exodus of the wife from her husband's control into the world to use her maternal quality for the service of others and to demand rights for herself and her children. We want something better than Christmas carol-singing over little children born to woe, something better than wailing over human sufferings. We see that these are largely our own creation. We want to get up from kneeling on the stool of penitence and begin to control our destiny. Despite the mockery of the cynics, too, we want to give up hampering ourselves and torturing each other with jealousy and hatred disguised as morals and the law. We want to be members one of another in a sense the orthodox Christian will not understand.

Modern people realise that this means closer concern for the economic welfare of each other. This is why no step can be taken without some measures for abolishing wide disparity of incomes. It implies the use of child nurture and education as a levelling process in society. That this may be done we must attempt to obtain widespread acceptance of new social beliefs and educational theories. Further, since pioneer work in education is at the moment ahead of the average level, we must bring up the average before crystallisation happens.

We would like each child to have a new start in a new world; that he should take pride, not in his origins, but in friendships and the achievements of himself and his friends. To this end he should be liberated from his ancestors, who drag upon him, as the heavy tails of prehistoric monsters impeded their movement and threatened their extinction.

But is it not the family and the heredity it implies that safeguard individual liberty? In setting the child free from this, do we not prepare for him a worse slavery in the Servile State or in a machine-made society? This is an objection that is usually heard from those who, in our present State, are in a position of privilege. Curiously they are unaware of how little liberty is accorded to those less fortunate than they. Certainly we risk a new slavery, for this risk will always be present so long as human beings need any government at all. But it does not look to me so bad as the insecurity and despairing aimlessness that we now endure. The new social sanctions will be different from the old, but they will have to command acceptance. To this degree the individual will not be irresponsibly free. He will start as a child from his own desires, building his personality in association with peers of his own age. At each stage he will have to act both as an individual with needs and as a social person respecting the needs of others. He will not, if his environment is soundly adjusted, have been put upon by authority either from adults or elder brothers and sisters or from teachers. Equally he will not have been pampered by them into arrested development. He should therefore, when he becomes adult, neither expect to serve slavishly nor to domineer.

May not this be the sound preparation for really *living* democracy, instead of talking about it? May it not be the way to get rid of the apathy produced by the social hierarchy under which we now live? And thus the way to a fuller and more real use of individual powers? Obviously, if we educate wrongly, we cannot produce this result. It may be better that few should be free, than that all should be slaves. But suppose that *all* can be free and that education can help them to freedom? Then, indeed, the way we handle the child's early development is the clue to the whole future.

There is a serious risk that a classless State will regard the child as a docile instrument, just as his parents did. As a safeguard against this, the technique of giving freedom to children has been repeatedly emphasised in this book. People will not cease to want power, even if they no longer exercise it through parenthood and religion. We must try at all costs not to let the State become the only power symbol. Power must be identified not as the holding of authority, nor the getting and keeping of wealth, but as power to control inanimate life and to avert danger in the service of human beings. The power urge must be thrown into the factory wheels, along the electric cable; it must soar with the pacific aeroplane, stand at the elbow of the bacteriologist, inspire the hands of the surgeon, the night-watches of doctors, nurses and all engaged on expert maternity.

When our pessimists are not talking of the Servile State, they tell of the triviality and licence that will come of sexual freedom. But our new society will be dealing, as we hope, with people who have not been goaded to revolt by repression nor so moulded by the family that they will play spoiled sons and daughters when they fall in love. They will perhaps handle sex as fun when they are growing up; and later use it for serious romantic friendships in which each tests the quality of the other's personality. For every child they bring into the world, whether in permanent or temporary partnership, social morality will hold them responsible. At the same time permitting them not to bear. If they are not rich and something is demanded from them for the children's keep, they will be likely to breed responsibly. Especially if such an attitude is implicit in the social ethic they have learned. Serious concern for children is likely to be implicit in a community that provides the greater part of their maintenance. Nor are women, at any rate so long as they must carry children in their own bodies, likely to have them unless they seriously want them.

In any sound system of society, of course, marriage or sex will not be open to women as a career. Women will be expected to help their lovers when they are in difficulty, just as their lovers help them. In the life of both children and adults the needs of their neighbours will be ever present and loyalties will not be restricted to blood relations. I believe that there will be more responsible action in love, rather than less, when our bad laws are cleared away. Perhaps too much responsibility, indeed, to please the men and women who use the present system for their profit and their pleasure.

Are we then to turn propagandist towards the children? Shall we create a bias towards this society of the future? This is a difficult problem. Some people feel that they can no longer honestly teach the old ideas and at the same time are diffident about imposing new doctrines. It is hard on young people to grow up in utter confusion. The results of not teaching the new may be that they will in the end simply be caught by the old. We who have seen the mediaeval world break down are frightened of a new rigidity. But we cannot study history without seeing that epochs of synthesis are needed by humanity, whatever their dangers. I think we do our children wrong if we do not try to let them know the forces that we believe may guide the future. The modern child should not be shut away from biology and psychology nor from social theory any more than from the radio and the motor-car. Since we teach him what has been discovered about sex and his own body, we must let him know, when he is ready, what we can tell of child-rearing and of marriage. We can let him learn from our mistakes. He will become aware, anyhow, of our confusion. Forbid nothing unless we absolutely must. Censor nothing, conceal nothing. Let him know himself and his own powers. He must make the world in which he is to live. It is we who must set him free from the past.

Part Four

EL SOL

1926–1930

During the late 1920s and early 1930s Dora Russell wrote a regular
feature for this Spanish periodical – on issues which, in her own
words, many of the English preferred not to hear. A selection has
been made from this extensive contribution and is followed by a list
of titles of many of the other articles. The articles were written in
English but published in Spanish. The original English versions are
published here.

SOCIAL BEHAVIOUR

Most of us who consider that we are civilised people are apt to reflect constantly on the uncivilised state of the world, and to despise our rulers for their incompetence. We wonder why the nations continue on the path of barbarism, and why nobody can be persuaded to take an interest in disarmament. As the worried and weary head-mistress of an entirely new school only a week old, I can only feel that it is surprising that there is any civilisation in the world at all. I have spent the past week in assisting and observing twenty young children whose ages range from two and a half to seven and a half attempting to live together in a democratic community for the first time. A great many of them are only children, this being the reason why they are under my care. Most of them have been either pampered or repressed by the constant companionship of adults. Their follies are often almost incredible, and their cruelties amazing. Quite big children cannot do up their buttons, and complain that they cannot get into their undergarments when they have forgotten to unbutton them. Small girls stand and roar with laughter when they see a bigger boy crying because he has fallen and hurt himself rather badly – the hurt being self-evident in cut knees. I blame none of these children, I am observing and learning. I note the parents' mistakes, and I try to keep track of my own. I observe the bad traits the children have acquired unnecessarily by wrong handling, side by side with those which are obviously due to natural and untamed egoism. To melt the ego, or to prevent it from ever hardening unduly is the fundamental problem of personal, social and international relationships. I have always held that this must be solved in the nursery or the school before the age of seven, and the toil of the past week confirms this belief up to the hilt. One only boy of seven here brought toys of his own, which he would allow no one to touch. He pushed and hit others when they wanted any of the communal school things that he wanted. We protected the very young ones and stood by to watch the situation. Presently the whole of the older group turned upon the offender and outlawed him. They did not hit, they merely mocked and criticised. He has had a hard time and in his turn he needs protection. But he is becoming a social being. At two years old, he could have learned all that with less pain and less bitter memories. But he could not have learned it from adults, least of all from his parents.

The kind parents are often the worst offenders, especially if they have only one child. So many of these children have been taught – and rightly so – to expect personal freedom and kindly treatment for themselves, but they have never expected to give the same consideration to others. The well meaning modern parent, when John or Jane does not eat the food provided, does not slap, but coaxes. The little ego swells with pride and step by step the adult is driven to giving more and more attention and emotional energy. I have children here who cannot bear it if a teacher speaks to any other child but themselves. They break in 'say it to me too' even if the attention given to the other child has been a reproof. It is not, as the psycho-analyst might say, that such children want to be scolded, because they are masochists – they want to be noticed that their egoism may be satisfied. Nothing the adult can do or say will make those children into social beings so rapidly or so painlessly as to live and sleep and eat in the company of a dozen others of their own age. It then becomes so obvious that one cannot receive all the attention, and that to sit crying into one's dinner plate is folly when the other children have finished and gone out to play. With nearly all of the children here there will be weeks and it may be months of work to break away the crust of posing and posturing that over-indulgent adults have let them build. In work as in eating and dressing and undressing, the same causes are operative. The adult must suggest and minister to the children constantly. They are intellectually, morally and even physically lazy. None of it is their own fault. Parents or nurses have either forbidden or done too much for them. Even these young ones are already – as I observe from their conversation – dependent on the shops, cinemas, expeditions here and there for their happiness and pleasure. I hope that before long the boredom of a country environment will drive them to learning and doing on their own initiative.

Obviously I am dealing in my group with the children of intelligent parents, who are not poor, and who have loved the children almost too well. If we could take children from the numerous families of the poor, our problems would be different – they would not be less, nor would they be any easier to solve. Kicks and cuffs or spoiling of a different kind would have unsuited them for co-operation or for work planned and executed by themselves. And these are the very qualities demanded by a democratic society – the power to work as an individual, and the power to live with one's fellow creatures. It is easy to be a moral and intellectual slave; it is easy to live with one's superiors or inferiors; easy to toady and flatter; easy to bully and oppress. But it is not easy to respect your equal, to help him work, to share with him the good food and playthings. Yet this can be learnt almost in the cradle, and once learnt at all universally, democracy would be a real possibility instead of the sham that it is to-day. I do not ask intelligent parents to send their children to my school. I merely suggest that they have at least two children of ages near to one another, and that they inculcate kindness and rational pacifism, without ever striking the children, before the children are four years old.

LABOUR WOMEN THINK FOR THEMSELVES

It is a remarkable experience for anyone who did not much believe in giving women votes to see a big Conference of political women in action. Women in England have had the franchise now since 1918 – and then only the women over thirty years of age, and not all of them, since domestic servants and women living with their parents cannot always qualify. In the short time which has passed since 1918, all the political parties have organised women's congresses. Early this month the Liberal women met, and on the eleventh and twelfth of May the Labour women held a great gathering at Huddersfield. As one left the railway station and came into the square, one realised immediately that something was going on. The whole square was filled with enormous motor charabancs, and they were filled to overflowing with laughing and cheering women. I suppose there were twelve or fifteen cars, and I only saw one man, except for the drivers. They were going out for an evening ride after the day's deliberations, over the wild moors of Yorkshire. One or two of the cars burst tires, and parties returned late and cold, but nothing could damp their happy enthusiasm. The women were of all ages, and of all types; some were young girls of working class origin, strong and exquisitely beautiful, speaking with the soft broad accents of the mill areas in the North, others were young middle class enthusiasts, and a few were Trade Union organisers, tired and worried by their perpetual battle on behalf of sweated women workers, but the vast majority were solid housewives and mothers, in middle years, round and matronly, or pinched, hungry and care-worn – not beautiful if you are looking for superficial delights, but lovely to the eyes of those who read courage, wisdom, love, energy and honesty in the lines of a face, or the movements of hands and body.

These women are interested in all problems. They listened to speeches on China with as keen attention as they gave to birth control – the most striking feature of the women is always what might least be expected by their critics, namely their concentrated attention to business. There is less fooling and waste of time on the whole than at the men's assemblies. But apart from general questions, it is evident that there are some matters of special interest to women. The Liberal women dealt with maternity endowment and birth control; similarly the Labour women dealt with these subjects, but in a more drastic fashion. They also added to their interests one which touches the middle-class liberal woman much less, the position of women employed in industry, and the provisions for them in unemployment and sickness.

The great debate of the Conference was that in which Miss Margaret Bondfield sought to defend herself for signing a recent report – the Blanesburgh Report – on unemployment benefit. Under this report the unemployed will be treated with greater severity than ever, benefit will be unjustly taken away and cut down. Young women out of work are to live on eight shillings a week. The Labour Party, with certain reservations, had accepted the report, as being the best they could get out of the present government. But the women would have none of it. By an overwhelming majority, they censured Miss Bondfield; who faced them with pluck and some anger. Another Trade Union woman supporting the report, was booed. The face of the Party chairman, Mr Roberts, who was watching the Conference, was good to see. How dare the Advisory Conference of Women advise anything contrary to what had already been decided for them by men? There is no doubt that the sufferings of the lock-out last year have so stiffened the women's resistance that they are now in many respects fiercer and more determined than the men.

To those who think that the rule of women will lead to puritanical repression, the attitude of the women on sex questions will come as a surprise. Their attitude on giving birth control advice at Public Maternity Centres has already become world famous; this year they re-affirmed the decision in spite of the knowledge that the leaders of the party are against them and in spite of three forcible speeches in opposition. These speakers were heard in silence, the women having some difficulty in restraining themselves, as two of the speakers were spinsters. 'You try it and see' muttered the women round me when a spinster woman doctor explained that the ninth confinement was so much easier than the first. On the question of sex offences against young girls, the women showed balanced judgment. They asked that the age at which a girl can 'consent' to sex be raised to seventeen, but refused to raise it to eighteen, because at that age girls are out freely at work, and may have sex relations with men whom they intend to marry. As a speaker put it, in these days we do not blame the men more than the girls, and free women do not want protection. When it is remembered that these are not young women who made this decision, it is clear what immense progress has been made on this subject. The older feminists meant the equal standard to mean more virtue for men; the young ones mean it to be more freedom for women – and they have actually converted their own mothers to their point of view. I know this to be true, from my own wide experience of speaking to Labour women on such topics. They quote their daughters with pride – because they have dared and achieved what they themselves longed for.

Those who want to know what women mean to the community and the future, could not do better than take a visitor's ticket to hear the Labour women. Listening to Conservative ladies is all very well, but it is only at such assemblies as this at Huddersfield that you can find industrial women, teachers, doctors, mothers who do their own housework, women clerks, and inspectors – all the women whose services count – meeting together to decide what they will do, now that they have power ultimately to enforce anything they please.

WOMEN DON'T THINK

This entertaining proposition is constantly being advanced by some propagandist or other. It is a very old and convenient assertion, so one may expect it to die hard. Only very recently in the world's history, and on certain parts of the world's surface, have we women even been allowed souls. Personally, I don't find a soul much advantage, but some women like to claim their rights in this respect. However that may be, I believe that in India and Moslem countries, and in old China, women have still no souls. Jewish women are excluded from religious worship, which they watch from a secluded gallery, as Englishwomen used to watch the sacred proceedings of their lords and masters in Parliament. I scarcely wonder that some of these female visitors sighed profoundly for a right to sit there, in order that for once the august assembly might hear a little common sense. Even that revolutionary bulwark of the Parliamentary system the English seventeenth century poet John Milton, champion of democracy against the Divine right of Kings, upheld the Divine right of men when he wrote 'He for God only, she for God in him'.

But now another English author called Mr. F. E. Baily has been letting himself go on the subject. At least he has courage, for, in a paper run by an organization of able business and professional women, he tells us that women think only with their emotions; that they have a weakness for crimes of passion; that only sexless academic women can begin to be impartial; that they would like to hang people who are cruel to animals; and that if women had been in men's privileged position in marriage they would have been too selfish to modify the divorce laws in favour of men.

It's queer, but there seem to have been hundreds of years

of torturing unfaithful wives before it occurred to rational males that the laws should be equal for both. And I never before heard a man admit that he held the privileged position in our marriage laws – indeed haven't men been screaming at us for ages that marriage was designed to protect us helpless creatures against their wickedness? They can't have it both ways.

And crimes of passion: the approval which greeted and caused to be acquitted returned soldiers who shot the lovers of unfaithful wives did not proceed from feminine lips – unless indeed from these *so* impartial and *so* sexless spinsters.

On cruelty to animals, I plead guilty. I would like to do the same back to anyone who wantonly hurts a living thing. I attribute this not to my sexual impulses, but to a maternal sympathy for all things whose substance is flesh and blood. Just so; all women think emotionally. In fact everybody thinks emotionally – that is why the quality and character of early acquired emotions is so important.

The present society is as much the expression of masculine emotions as a woman-created society would be of feminine ones. On many subjects men and women feel alike; where they do not, it is valuable that women should have the power to make their feelings count. Out of the tug of war between the ways of feeling perhaps impartiality will emerge. For example: the present English government propose to cut down public expenditure through local authorities. But there is the special provision that money from the Central Road Fund will be given to help in repairing and improving roads. Lady Astor – and she will have the support of women of all parties in this – will move an amendment that the public maternity and child welfare services shall be similarly promised some special exemption. Now, no one denies that roads may be important, but a road can stand neglect for a year or so, but if you don't feed a baby for a year it is rather unfortunate. I am sure Lady Astor, as a wealthy woman, is a keen motorist. I am not, none the less she would probably be at one with me on the issue *Roads versus babies*, whereas a man of her party would not. Both of us evidently can't think for sentiment; yet I suspect something childishly selfish and sentimental in the morbid passion of elderly male motorists for immaculately smooth roads. In fact in one London borough where the infant and maternal mortality rate was higher than the average, the Council accounts showed vast sums expended on paving the squares in rich and childless quarters; a mere pittance on health work; and nothing at all on providing an open place for the children to play, although there was absolutely none for them. To me at least it seems that the emotional bias of maternal women in these matters is going to be a valuable social and political asset. We feel that mothers and children have come off too badly in the past, but our emotional thinking by no means stops short at ourselves and our own children. We have feelings about the sacrifice of men in war, which we propose no longer to disregard as women's tears, but to translate into thoughts and deeds. We have views on the education of children, on the food supply, on sex relationships. We have even dared to think, here let us speak softly, of abolishing the home. In all of these causes we are prepared to do considerable hard thinking and hard fighting, in which mockery of our irrational emotionalism will ever be a favourite weapon of our opponents.

It is curious how tenaciously men cling to the theory that women are neither realistic nor rational. Like men we have a romantic period in adolescence, but then we grow up, and they so often don't especially if they have one of us to protect them from hard details. Maternity – for one must consider this mainly, it being the essential fact which divides woman from man – makes us executive and practical. Possibly we do not think for thinking's sake quite so often as men, but this is an asset in political and social action. We deal in real problems, and we want real solid solutions. It is easy to embark on fantastic national adventures to distract people; it is hard to do all the dull detailed work necessary to organise for individual and social happiness. 'To grapple effectually', wrote Joseph Conrad (who appreciated his wife's cooking), 'with purely material problems requires more serenity of mind and more lofty courage than people generally imagine'.

This peculiar ability has been woman's since first society was stable and there were any domestic arts. Valuable to her family her skill and foresight are as valuable in the wider field of the modern state. To say that the intuitive and manipulative type of skill involved in weaving, sewing, cooking, nursing, teaching young children, loving and helping people – is not thinking, is to commit the typical error of a society which still repeats the measurement of intelligence evolved by scholastic theologians and medieval monks who dreaded woman as the enemy of salvation.

THE ENGLISH GENTLEMAN

I suppose that an English writer who is asked for a series of articles for Spanish readers must be expected to give, so far as possible, a picture of England and English life. The view which people in one country have of another is generally so very different from that which presents itself to the people in the country itself. When an Englishman thinks of Spain, he has at once a vague picture of orange trees laden with shining fruit, of the misty green foliage of olive trees lining the horizon, of women in bright shawls dancing, or of men riding about like Don Quixote, their long legs dangling across mules with coloured harness and jingling bells. Does the Spaniard when he thinks of England have visions of a fat John Bull, or of scarlet coated huntsmen chasing a cheerful fox, or is it factory chimneys belching smoke, grimy men in blue overalls, or the vast steel arches of our station roofs, the sleek efficiency of the engines that draw our great Expresses that make England romantic to the Spanish reader if he dreams of England at all?

The significance and power of England in this and the last century are undoubtedly wrapped up in her industrial areas, and yet the well-to-do, the literary or the artistic Englishman not only never visits these areas, but scarcely ever gives them a thought except when strikes or rumours of strikes trouble the fair prospect of the Ascot race meeting, or threaten the non-delivery of the morning milk upon the townsman's doorstep. Our novelist, Arnold Bennett, whose youth knew the dreary monotony of the Five Towns – the pottery districts in the middle of England where most of our china and hardware are made – tried in a play a few years back to draw a satirical contrast between the 'industrial

North' and the frivolous South which holds the reins of power and Government and provides the main playground of the rich; in fact between the region which makes smooth white baths and silver taps and the people that lie in them luxuriously in the morning taking the Englishman's boasted daily bath. (This bath, by the way, is only enjoyed by an infinitely small number of our population.) Mr Bennett's play *The Bright Island* was not successful, but the idea which it tried to embody is in England a constant and menacing truth. The recent General Strike was in fact a struggle between these two parts of our kingdom.

First then, let us make a portrait of our ruling Englishman, not because he is the most important, but because he is at the moment, the most powerful. Mr Baldwin, our Prime Minister, is the perfect type. Educated at Harrow, one of the big public schools for gentlemen, he became rich through the labours of men in the iron and steel trade. None the less, he thinks that England is great because the soil of his home county Worcestershire is red, and because the hay smells good when they cart it home on summer evenings. When a successful manufacturer says this, smoking his English pipe with a meditative air, the landed gentry forget and acclaim him a national hero, as one of themselves, the backbone of England. They forget that neither he nor they ever tossed hay or milked a cow in their lives and that the majority of their fellow countrymen have never smelt hay or seen soil unpolluted by the smoke and cinder heaps of factories and mines.

Then Mr Baldwin has the right face for the part. Probably in youth his chin was solid and firm, nose straight like the young Englishmen depicted on our popular magazines, healthy, bright, energetic, with a comfortable air of stupidity. In middle years Mr Baldwin shows the right development – chin broad and plump, nose now somewhat fleshy, a ruddy well-fed complexion. Simple, sturdy, virtuous, just, the very man so everybody exclaims, to steer his country through a time of crisis. Luckily he learnt a little Latin at school – not much else – and so he can make play with Roman words and Roman virtues and an air of disinterested culture. Behold our steel magnate well equipped to play therefore, draped in his exquisite camouflage, a modern Cinnatus rising to save his people from a non-existent plough. No one will take this innocent seeming merchantman for a ship of war! And with what childish simplicity the people accept him, women's hearts are touched, they write to the Liberal papers proclaiming that at the very mention of his name we should all rise and stand in silence. (It might be a good plan to do this in Parliament to stop the passage of his iniquitous bills.) But no, such sarcasm is unworthy. The Labour leaders proclaimed the virtue of this gentleman, they were proud to shake him by the hand. Now the spider pounces, the false bulwarks go down, the guns are trained. The miners' children starve, their fathers will work longer hours, their wages will be less, their rights of protest curtailed. Marvellous English gentlemen, how nobly you break strikes, joy-riding in people's motorcars, how bravely you forgo your warm baths in summer that the miners may submit. It is easier, of course, than volunteering for the mines. How splendidly you purge the common people of that wicked foreign influence which makes them sigh for things no Englishman who is not a gentleman should demand. How brilliantly you keep your word of honour – not of course to mere foreigners, Germans or the working class, but to men who were educated at your old school. For them and you and your children the lawns and gardens and sun-bathed hay fields, for the rest of the world whatever is left, for your workpeople and their children the hovels and the ashpit. Perhaps the Spanish reader, if not you, will be interested if I describe these people who serve and whom, because you are rich and powerful, you despise.

THE AWAKENING PEASANT

It is a commonplace now in sociological thinking to contrast the old agricultural or peasant ways of thought with the more modern industrial or urban attitude. This was, however, not the case some ten years ago, and it is only recently that serious attention has been given to the profound changes in human thinking which are brought about by economic habits and daily occupations.

In this connection I have lately been reading two novels – one Gladkov's *Cement* which depicts the life of Russian peasants and workers since the Revolution, the other Liam O'Flaherty's *House of Gold* which deals with the Irish country people since the Sinn Fein movement which brought about the independence of Ireland.

I have always been struck by the similarity between the Welsh and Irish temperament and that of the Russians or Poles. It is a real effort for the Nordic, that is to say, for the English, or North European temperament, to establish any *rapport* with the Slav or the Celt; we feel them to be so often extravagant and inhumane, they look upon us as unimaginative, stupid, practical. It is an amusing reflection, none the less, that the Irish, for all the boasted poetical temperament of their people, have never produced the same amount or degree of really great poetry as stands to the credit of us unimaginative English. To me it appears that the poetical nature of the Irish, as to some extent that of the Russian, belongs to the faery world of fantasy and unreality. To feel poetry the Irishman must forget certain unpleasant things about real life, he cannot feel it as part of life's texture, brutal though life may be. In this respect Shakespeare is the supreme example of the English poet, who can, when he chooses, invest every part of life, even the mean or the cruel, with poetic glory. Yeats, and even Bernard Shaw are typically Irish – there are always for them certain things in life which are too ugly to be other than ignored or despised. Especially is this true of things which have to do with sex, or the body. Shaw for instance in *Methuselah* represents as an important part of his millennium, revolutionary changes in the mechanism of human digestion and reproduction. In this he is following in the wake of some of the more finicking medieval mystics, such as Pierre Bayle, who took pleasure in satirising, in the improper footnotes of his Dictionary. And to the Irish lover, more than to any other, it is necessary to think of his lady as a fairy or an angel, her bodily processes, more especially the distortions and agonies of maternity, he would prefer to ignore.

It may be merely that the Irish have been more deeply impressed with, and are more tenacious of the medieval outlook than are more modernized nations, for certainly the influx of modern views in revolutionary Russia is having a profound effect upon the Russian attitude to the whole of life; and the interesting fact about the contrast between the two books I have mentioned is that where both are dealing with a somewhat similar state of society as regards economic and historical development, their big assumptions about men and women and society are poles asunder. O'Flaherty shows how now that the English landlord is eclipsed in the Irish countryside and the English imperial power no longer has prestige, the poorer peasantry are either living like beasts on what they can wring from small holdings, or are being exploited by petty capitalists – bigger farmers, traders, like the Russian Kulak or the Nep men – who are without concern for the country as a whole or for any values apart from their own money hoard. In the background are a few well-meaning people who begin to talk of helping the peasants by co-operatives, while round about and burnt into the people's lives is the power of the priesthood. The people are interested only in their beasts, in drink, in women and in petty thieving; their superstitions prevent them either from thinking or hoping. The drama of the book circles around a beautiful golden-haired woman, both a part and a symbol of the golden hoard which the local capitalist, her brutal husband, holds. The priest, the doctor, a young peasant, her husband all desire her – she does no wrong other than to love the young peasant, yet she is represented as the golden snake, evil incarnate, the curse of the village. The priest rapes her – and murders her. The husband murders him and then dies. The peasants continue to drink and to suffer, and no one has the courage openly to support any scheme for social betterment. It is a terrible, tragically hopeless book, the more so when one perceives how the tragedy is rooted in out-worn ideas and beliefs about men and women, sin, and religion which are coiled like snakes at the heart of the people so that they cannot get free.

How much more freely one breathes in Gladkov's atmosphere. Here is a book which contains plenty that is cruel, awful, outrageous – men and women torturing each other's souls and bodies by flogging, starving, slaying; men breaking down women's resistance to their sexual advances by violence – but through it all shines the magnificence of the struggle to create *new* men and women and a new society. The people of a country district with a large factory are trying in the face of raids from Cossacks, lack of technical knowledge and deliberate sabotage from surrounding peasantry, to get their factory going again after the revolutionary wars. The women have collected the young children into creches and homes and battle like tigresses to keep them from disease and starvation. The men look in vain to their Communist wives for the personal submission and service that was theirs in the old family days. But they are trying to learn that women are no longer slaves, nor evil, and some of the loveliest passages of the book are those in which young husbands and wives struggle to understand not only each other's infidelities but their hardness and indifference to each other at the call of the need of society as a whole. And the humour and the sorrow that pervade the scene of the expulsions from the Party! The sense of the Russian countryside, the weather, of bitter loss at the slipping of some comfortable animal way of behaviour which they dimly feel the machine that they admire has come to destroy. This, one feels, is life as Shakespeare saw it, shirking nothing, attempting all. And such a race, breaking out of the tyranny of priesthood and medieval thought have the vitality to bring abundant hope to themselves and to the modern world. If any country can create life whole under modern conditions Russia can.

MORALS A HUNDRED YEARS HENCE

There is never a time when we do not hear about the dreadful decay of morals, especially among the younger generation. If the pessimists are right, we must all have been getting steadily wickeder and wickeder for thousands of years, and our depravity will scarcely bear examination beside the pure fresh virtue of neolithic man. Optimists, on the other hand, tell us that we are innately virtuous and that our morals progress with time: – 'Only we know that man is an advancer, Only we know the centuries revolve.' (I don't know about man, but I am quite convinced that woman is an 'advancer' in our present age.) The optimists and the pessimists alike contradict themselves: for those who think us wicked always want us to go as far away as possible from our animal ancestry and traditions, whereas those who think us good, usually preach a 'return to nature', that is throwing away all the civilisation which our progressing virtue has built up through the ages.

I confess I am an optimist; though not one of those who regard bare feet and cave dwelling as essential to the good life. But I do believe that human morality, both public and private, is changing for the better and that at the present time the change is rapid all over the world. That is why I hope we may go fast enough to prevent the collapse of our present civilisation, because it contains the seeds of something probably better than the world has yet known.

That writers on morals are expected to deal mainly with sexual morality is the most severe condemnation of our traditional idea of virtue. We are so superstitious on this particular subject that we are willing to sacrifice dozens of more important virtues in order to keep our completely arbitrary marriage system intact. A hundred years hence, probably, no one will dream of starving or ill-treating or miseducating either the children or adults, and the whole idea of compelling people to love one another by legal, economic and social pressure will be regarded as simply silly. Biology and psychology will have shown us at last the way to educate people for social co-operation and happiness. Morals will be the expression of certain biological needs and sanctions, and education the science of directing rather than choking our important physical impulses and activities. People will realise that to be good human beings we must first of all be good animals; that is, we must have bodies perfect in health and beauty, trained and nourished from early youth to loveliness and vigour like the plants in a well-tended garden. The whole trend of modern education and social feeling is towards this as the first important achievement. Old-fashioned people think we are bulding on gross materialism, and neglecting necessary discipline and spiritual values. Yet by modern methods humanity is solving, daily and hourly, problems which the birch, the prison, war, and even religion, could not solve in hundreds of years. The work of Freud, Montessori and others has shown how much the mind and spiritual values are a product of environment and early exercise of the senses; physiology teaches how much the emotions depend on the functioning of the glands and parts of our body which, under the influence of asceticism, we have considered too horrid or animal to be mentioned still less studied. When we consider human beings as organisms an entirely new standard of morality will be evolved. Organic matter likes to spread, expand and create in its own likeness; morality will recognise these needs by a code based on the right of everyone to food, warmth, shelter, knowledge, sex and parenthood. No more in fact than we at present allow to our plants and domestic animals but deny to countless of our fellow creatures. What gardener would be so insane as to put a water-loving plant on a sun-baked mound and scold its lust for water as a mortal sin? A hundred years hence people will not say of others 'Are they virtuous?' i.e. do they go to chapel with gloves and an umbrella, pay their bills and live without passion with one husband or one wife? People will say rather

'Are they creative?' do they do their work with skill, grace
and intelligence, whether it be engineering, cooking, agriculture, or abstruse science; are their children as lovely as
the wit of man and woman combined with the help of the
community can make them? All this is quite regardless of
whether those children come into being in accordance with
our present notions of what is right and wrong. There will be
women who breed and tend children with exquisite art and
science, selecting their fathers – not by chilly eugenics alone
but also with the passion of an artist and a lover. Love will be
what it should be, the instrument of mutual understanding
between men and women, and jealousy, robbed of economic
sanctions, will tend to disappear among people reared to
freedom and generosity. Greed will be dealt with among the
very young by accustoming them to plenty and a fair division
with the others. Morals, in the light of modern science, is a
vast subject, embracing politics at home and abroad,
economics as well as medicine and education. A hundred
years hence, if our present miseducated rulers – poor infants
– do not smash everything in one of their childish rages, we
may have got so far as to realise that you can breed and
nurture man into marvellous loveliness, but that you will
achieve nothing so long as you continue to bludgeon him like
a slave.

EL SOL ARTICLES 1926—1930

Literature of Despair
The Woes of Intellectuals
Parenthood and Immortality
The Future of Morality
Is Rationalism a Failure?
On Charity
Holidays in Russia
On Living at Home
Modern Marriage
Labour in Office
Sinclair Lewis on Anglo-American Relations
What About Pacifism?
The Detective Story
Labour Women Display Unusual Patience
East Winds and Politics
Men and Women and Fashion
Women Don't Think
America and England
Children are the Sole Reason for Marriage
History and Poetic Vision
The Search for Beauty
On Taking Holidays
The English Outlook
Our American Conquerors
Are There Any Adults?
Mothers in Revolt
A Challenge to America's Faith in Success
The Importance of Being an Aristocrat
The World, the Flesh and the Devil
Social Behaviour

Women a Hundred Years Hence
Who Wants to Govern?
Masculine and Feminine Literature
Is the Labour Tide Ebbing?
Women and Trade Unionism
At the Labour Party Conference (1926)
Women and Trade Unions
The English Gentleman
Morals a Hundred Years Hence
Marriage and Freedom
Educating Girls
Honesty is the Best Policy
Masculine and Feminine
William Clissold's World
Labour Women Think for Themselves
Sinclair Lewis: *Elmer Gantry*
Care and Health of Children
Lindbergh's Flight
Will the Towns Conquer? (Fülop Millar on Bolshevism
   Machine Worship)
National Charade in Vulgar Amusements
The English Theatre Improves
On Abolishing the Home
Love of Money
What is Savagery?
A Labour Government Again?
A Woman Who Lived her Own Life (Isadora Duncan)
Stormy Times (Effect of Weather on Moods – Politics)
On Bishops
Sunday in Hyde Park
Why Not Abolish the Home?
A Glacial Epoch
Food and the Protestant Religion
The Merits of the Jews
Early Teaching of Music
Towards Mediocrity
The Awakening Peasant

Part Five

SUNDAY CHRONICLE
1933

Having made for herself a reputation as an educationalist and an enlightened mother, Dora Russell was offered by the Editor of the *Sunday Chronicle* the opportunity of writing a series of articles on child rearing for that paper. Her ideas were radical for the time, and while she was prepared to argue for the delights of motherhood (and the rights of women to engage in motherhood *without penalty*), she was neither a romantic nor a sentimentalist when it came to advising mothers on the rearing of their children. She had experienced the demands of children for herself and knew that women were often torn between meeting their own needs, and the needs of those who were dependent on them.

The first article in the series is included in order to give some indication of her writing at the time.

YOUR BABY
All He Will Need in His First Year

A great deal of sentiment surrounds the arrival of a new baby. To the parents their own child is wonderful and unlike any other.

In one sense this is true, since everyone is an individual. But it is also true that he is like every other child in that he will puzzle and disappoint his parents; and they are like all other parents in that they will make much the same sort of mistakes.

At first baby, if his mother has plenty of milk for him, is contented and will remain for some time unaware how much he is at the mercy of this complex world he has rashly entered.

WHAT MATTERS

But what is going to matter to him most? Undoubtedly it is the way his parents feel about him and the way they treat him.

Though nobody would deny that money has a direct and indirect influence, it is not so great as some may think in their moments of despair.

To the mother about to get on her feet and take over the new baby I want to say that no matter what the circumstances she and the baby's father can play a great part in making him happy and successful both in childhood and when he is grown-up.

Perhaps, though they hardly like to admit it, they did not really want him. It is too late to grieve over that now that he is here; they must try to put it right out of their mind. If they do not, the child is going to feel their indifference through

117

every little thing that they do for him.

Perhaps they did want him very much indeed; but his mother is inexperienced and finds there is more pain and slavery about having a baby than she had expected.

Again, this is her concern and not the baby's. It is a great cruelty to take out on a child the feelings of grown-up people with which he has nothing to do. Parents often do this without quite knowing it.

LEARN THE JOB

Even a tiny baby a few weeks old is not too young to feel his parents' moods. Loud noises and angry voices will startle him, and if his mother is irritable he will feel it through her haste and the touch of her hands when she attends to him.

If she is calm and smiling, he will be calm too, and will soon smile back.

Your baby is born. The best thing you can do now is to *learn* the job of creating a human personality, not assuming that you know all about it, as grandmother did.

The more trouble you are willing to take the less you will feel that it is trouble, because you will become absorbed in what is one of the most interesting jobs in the world.

Part Six

THE MINISTRY OF INFORMATION

During and just after the war, Dora Russell worked for the Ministry of Information, writing many reports – particularly those related to science – for publication in Russia. It was a time when Britain and Russia were allies and, partly because of this experience of co-operation and exchange between the East and the West, Dora Russell feels more keenly than most the destructiveness and the waste of the present relationships. More detailed accounts of this period of her life are contained in the most recent volume of her autobiography, *Tamarisk Tree Three*.

Part Seven

THE WOMEN'S CARAVAN OF PEACE

1958

Convinced that hostility was not inevitable and that it was possible to have a world peace, Dora Russell has been an active peace campaigner throughout her life. She has also had unwavering faith in women's capacity to cut across national boundaries and to promote peace. During the 1950s she was responsible for organising many a women's peace protest and in 1958 she led the Women's Caravan of Peace throughout the countries of Europe. Greenham Common, the current women's peace protest, builds upon the traditions which Dora Russell helped to establish. The following extracts are taken from her account of how she with many other women demonstrated that there is more to unite women in peace than to divide them by war.

THE TRAVELLERS

Jane Wyatt
Hilda Lettice
Edith Adlam
Doris Adams
Jo Warren
Jill Vasey
Rosalyn Popp
Paula Popp
Julia James
Helga Gininge
Dora Russell
Jane Saxby
Martha Fynn
Wynne Marshall
Sybil Cookson

CARAVAN
Edinburgh to Moscow Places Visited

Edinburgh
London: St. Paul's service
France
Belgium
Paris
Rheims
West Germany
Switzerland
Italy
Yugoslavia
Bulgaria
Rumania
Hungary
Poland
Moscow
East Germany
Dresden
Belgium
London: Hyde Park

WE CALLED ON EUROPE

Chapter 1 The Background to Our Story

More than twenty years have passed since the peoples of Europe celebrated their victory over Hitler's bid for totalitarian power. In all countries the deepest emotion in 1945 was relief from the intolerable threat of foreign domination, and with it came the hope of rebuilding national economies that would afford the basis of happiness and liberty for all.

But the years that followed brought disillusion. Hatred and suspicion, once unleashed, are difficult to bring once more under control. Human beings who have been maimed in mind and body by some of the most terrible sufferings ever endured by mankind, do not turn readily to peaceful reconstruction and good relations with their neighbours. Moreover, though only a very few had realised it, the legacy of this second world war was something far worse than the rubble of cities, devastated fields, blind, disfigured, crippled men and women, homeless refugees, orphaned children. This had been a total war; which compelled every citizen to participate. Against this concept of total war so many had fought, in the belief that, with the fall of Hitler, it would be destroyed. Only gradually did people begin to understand that the concept of total war, so far from being destroyed, had become a far greater menace, in that it had gripped the imagination of the World's statesmen. Henceforth, any war would be a total war. To crown all, the scientists of many nations, torn apart by the Warring Chieftains, had equipped total war with the ultimate weapons – the 'A' and then the 'H' bomb.

These men of science, like their colleagues in literature and the arts, had looked forward to peace as an end to secrecy and division, to the renewal of discussion with their colleagues in other countries, in which each man or woman would be able to state an opinion freely and frankly. Such individual liberty could not be tolerated under the concept of total war. Each block or nation must be firmly welded together, in order that, in the event of war, they would act as one. It was essential that people should be prevented from beginning even to like one another again. Therefore all the resources of the mass media, press, radio, television, the cinema, were turned to the purpose of keeping alive fear and suspicion. Within nations the witch hunt also began. Complete conformity with the Establishment became essential to advance in most careers; national and ideological prejudice infected the judgment of books or works of art, the cold war invaded even the realm of sport.

People from practically every country of Europe had suffered and died in Nazi concentration camps; it was, ultimately, the unity of these peoples which had won the war. The natural sequence should have been a greater European unity, which would have meant a great deal to the world. Instead the cold war split Europe in half. Consequently since 1945 there has not been a single day of respite from actual war, and from the fear that the smaller wars in progress could lead to a major conflagration.

In this atmosphere the younger generations have been growing to manhood and womanhood. Most of those now in their teens have never known anything but this state of war-like tension, the incessant propaganda for nationalism, the 'way of life' or particular orthodoxy of the society in which they live. In some countries they have been familiarised more and more with violence, brutality and belligerence by means of the cinema, radio and television. Their young minds have been warped by lies, and half-truths, their spontaneous generous emotions dammed at source or diverted imperceptibly into channels of hatred and suspicion of their fellow-creatures. The traditional accepted training in good social behaviour within the family and in school was thus in sharp conflict with the world as presented to them by those who control information and opinion. Split minds, delinquency, anxiety states, sometimes leading to mental illness, have resulted.

It is not possible to recount here in detail all the efforts of the more far-sighted men and women in Europe and beyond to rouse the peoples to an understanding of the danger, frustration and mental servitude to which the concept of total war condemned them. One might have expected that men of science, whose work was by tradition a strong international force, would have begun to lead the way towards sanity. By what right, some began to ask, had the scientists allowed their brilliant discoveries to be prostituted to war and the nuclear bomb? The reactions of a few eminent scientists immediately the war ended are of interest. Sir Henry Dale, then President of the Royal Society of Britain, whose foundation principle in the 17th Century was the use of the 'new philosophy' for the good of mankind, began well by a letter to *Nature* protesting against the security and secrecy in which science was now imprisoned. There was need, he said, to set science free, even if the attempt should lead to persecution, such as had been the fate of Galileo and Giordano Bruno. Subsequently, Sir Henry resigned his honorary membership of the Soviet Academy of Sciences on the Lysenko issue, in which he held that political considerations had overruled the objectivity of science. But he did not pursue the corresponding tactics as regards the increasing subservience of science to politics in the West.

Little more was heard of scientists courting martyrdom for freedom, though the action of Fuchs, in giving away secrets pertaining to the H bomb, for which he served a long sentence, must, I think, be so regarded in a historical perspective, whatever the view taken of his act by his contemporaries. For this was a case in which a man set his loyalty to human knowledge above loyalty to the interests of one nation.

The whole question of policy in regard to scientific secrets had, even while the war was in progress, been dictated by cold war tactics. The discoveries of the atom bomb, the jet engine, radar, penicillin were freely communicated by the British to America, but not to their other ally, the Soviet Union.

Although, as is now known, many of the American

scientists who helped to make the atom bomb, did make very earnest representations to their Government against its use, and Oppenheimer fell into disfavour later, for advising against proceeding to the H bomb, most scientists at first disclaimed or avoided political responsibility.

At a meeting of the British Association for' the Advancement of Science, just as the war ended, Sir Edward Appleton, then at the head of the Department of Scientific and Industrial Research, stated that he did not think the scientist should be held responsible for the results outside his laboratory of the discoveries which he made within it. Opposition to this view from the floor, however, met with hearty applause.

Many leading members of the Association of Scientific Workers in Britain, such as Professor Bernal, Professor Blackett, Sir Robert Watson Watt, Sir Julian Huxley; and such men as Dr Brock Chisholm (later at the head of the World Health Organisation), did not, even at the outset, agree that the scientist could be absolved of moral and social responsibility. J. G. Crowther, too, took the initiative in starting the World Federation of Scientists in an attempt to begin to re-unite scientific opinion.

But in the main, it was left to ordinary citizens to take the first steps in a campaign against the bomb and the cold war. Many organisations, in the national and international scale, were, of course, constantly active for peace – the National Peace Council, the Peace Pledge Union in Britain, the Women's International League for Peace and Freedom, the Co-operative women, nationally and internationally, the World Federation of United Nations. But none of these, in effect, stepped across the barrier set in their path by the cold war. It is thus essential to stress the work of those who sought to face this issue squarely and to go to the heart of the matter.

The first large scale manifesto against the arch enemy, the nuclear bomb, which saw the birth of the World Peace Council, was the Stockholm appeal of 1949, supported by hundreds of millions. The attempt to hold the first World Peace Congress in 1950 at Sheffield in Britain, failed on account of the refusal of the Labour Government to grant the necessary visas. The Congress moved to Warsaw and this movement was driven towards the East. The efforts of its peacemakers were smeared and decried, news of their activities with-held as far as possible from the mass of the people in many countries. Peace became, and still is, a dirty word. None the less, ordinary men and women were beginning to recover their sanity and tolerance and to grow tired of the posturing of Statesmen. The Vienna Peace Congress of 1952, with its very large delegations from Western Europe, was perhaps the turning point, when the tides of hatred at last began to recede. This was the more remarkable, since the Korean War, which began in 1950, had aroused violent passions.

In 1954 the Women's International Democratic Federation, another body which had started in the West, in Paris, and been driven eastwards, and which had held, none the less, consultative status at the United Nations since the foundation of that organisation, was deprived of that status, on the initiative of the United States and Great Britain, for its action in sponsoring a Commission of women from 20 countries, which visited North Korea, called attention to the devastation there and appealed for an end to the war. Many of the women who took part in this delegation were victimised in their respective countries, and the Women's International Democratic Federation has, so far, never been restored to status at the UN.

Next came a very important move from the scientists. Late in 1954 or early 1955, when Britain was making her strange contribution to peace by the decision of her Government to make the H bomb, scientists of East and West, on the initiative of Bertrand Russell and Einstein, published their famous manifesto warning the world of the appalling dangers of nuclear weapons. Later, this was followed by the meeting of East and West Commonwealth scientists at Pugwash, at which the theme was further developed. These statements received practically no publicity in national papers.

But among the intellectuals, certainly among those better equipped than the average citizen to understand the dangers, anxiety was increasing. Women especially were alarmed. I recall that at a Congress of women of all classes from all over India in 1954, the bulk of the resolutions handed up in many languages and on odd torn scraps of paper, were against the bomb. The effects of the American tests in the Pacific, the fate of the Japanese fishermen, the delayed results of the Hiroshima bomb, could no longer be completely concealed.

The Japanese scientists and people, setting up their Council Against the Atomic Bomb, sought to warn the world by means of the facts of their own appalling experience. Presently, the Windscale incident in Britain, which rendered radio-active milk and food stuffs over a very considerable area, brought the lesson nearer home.

The World Congress of Mothers, of over a thousand women, also bridging East and West, met in Lausanne in 1955 and set up the Permanent International Committee of Mothers, who issued their Declaration of Mothers for the Defence of Children against War in 1956. A letter from myself on the subject, published in the (London) *Observer*, brought a response from five hundred women all over the country in a few days.

The World Peace Council had continued its work steadily since 1950, as also had the numerous societies, founded in several countries, to promote friendship and cultural relations with communist peoples. All were hampered in their work by the constant cold war on communism, and in Britain especially, by the ban on membership imposed by the Labour Party. All these organisations have, with some justice, been reproached with pursuing too narrowly a communist line, but it is difficult to see what other result could have been expected, if those of different persuasions were forbidden to join or scared into not doing so. But the fact remains that these societies did, and are still doing, good service in keeping open the channels between East and West and their work has been instrumental in promoting the tourist traffic to Eastern Europe, which now begins to gather momentum.

The situation outlined above, must be taken into account, since it explains to a large extent the slowness of the West to show a stronger initiative against the threat of nuclear war.

To the younger generation in Britain must be given the credit for the first cracking of the ice. Students at the universities and young people in general were frequently accused by their elders of showing no interest in political questions. Looking back, one can see that this was due, almost entirely, to their objection to being imprisoned in the strait-jackets offered to them by existing political parties and other organisations. In the newly founded universities and Left Review Club in London spontaneous and free discussion suddenly broke loose. The hundreds flocking to it showed that it filled a deep need of the times.

Younger members of the Labour Party, on the initiative of the women, and with the support of sections of the Friends' Peace movement, started early in 1957 the Council for the Abolition of Nuclear Weapons. One of its first actions was the protest march of the women in May that year, which took place in pouring rain. It drew women from all classes and organisations; leading women and women MPs under the Chairmanship of Mrs Diana Collins (wife of Canon Collins), among them Vera Brittain, Mrs Joyce Butler MP, Dr Edith Summerskill MP, spoke in Trafalgar Square. Women in black picketed the lobby of the House of Commons, and, following a second march, with the adhesion of several very prominent people, among them J. B. Priestley, Sir Julian Huxley, the Campaign for Nuclear Disarmament was born, with Bertrand Russell as its President and Canon Collins its Chairman. As its name makes clear, the slogan of the Campaign was not pacifism, but the banning of the H bomb.

To the left of the Campaign, the Direct Action Committee, with Hugh Brock, Allen Skinner, the Rev. Michael Scott, Pat Arrowsmith and others, started operations and it was they who conceived the idea of the March to Aldermaston at Easter 1958, which the Campaign Committee, now known as the CND, decided to support. This was not, in fact, the first march to Aldermaston, for a small group of pacifists had already gone there to make a protest. And already in March 1958, the National Assembly of Women had organised in London the first women's conference against the H bomb.

The Permanent International Committee of Mothers had, in January 1957, made its protest to the United Nations by presenting its Declaration to the General Assembly and to the majority of the delegations from different countries in

New York. Only three of its twelve delegated members received visas from the United States Government. Among those refused was the widow of the Japanese fisherman who had died as the result of the Bikini test fall-out. Having done its best to make a gesture westwards, the Mothers' Committee was considering the possibility of an effort of West and East, to bring together against the threat of nuclear war, in some unusual way, the women and mothers of Europe. Already in the Autumn of 1957, as secretary of the Committee, I was thinking of a journey like a pilgrimage across Europe. The evident anxiety of women, the response to the Mothers' Declaration and the rising feeling in Britain against the H bomb, seemed to indicate that an initiative might possibly be taken from there. As I watched the growth of the CND, with its slogan of unilateral nuclear disarmament, it was clear that the West had, at long last, found a way to take an important step forward. How important this was to become, subsequent events have shown. Those who had been hampered by bans and restrictions were now able to come forward and express their protest.

But it was significant that this movement was then a purely national one, concentrating on the demand for a moral lead from one national Government. Many of those who took part in it had little or no knowledge, at first, of similar campaigns in other countries, or, indeed, of some in their own. The silence of press and radio had effectively impeded such movements and imprisoned them in the main within their own frontiers. It seemed to me that some symbolic act to break through frontier barriers was called for.

Accordingly, there came the idea that the women and mothers of Europe might act as pioneers in such an effort. We could at least plan and undertake our journey and see what results might flow from it. With the approval of the Committee of the Women's Co-operative Guild in England and Wales and the support of our Mother's Committee throughout Europe, the Women's Caravan of Peace came into being.

EPILOGUE

The final chapter of this book, as originally written in 1958, dealt with 'prospects and conclusions' on our return. It is long, and much of it deals with details of subsequent events within the peace movements and at international government level.

We met with the same blanket of silence in the Press and hostility from other organisations, as had been evident before we left. There was a mean attack by a certain section of the Press to discredit us personally, alleging vanity and frivolity on the part of the young women. Not being able to afford libel actions, we had to ignore this. We carried our banner throughout the Aldermaston March of 1959, and took part in any demonstrations by other organisations – (to which as individual members some of us belonged) – but which would not recognise our effort or publicise our story, or our film, which we made at the expense of one or two devoted people, all of which placed on record the similar movements in Europe and the earnest desire of communists also for peace. The CND movement was parochial, concentrating on the attempt, which ultimately failed, to convince the Labour Party on unilateral nuclear disarmament.

In 1959 it was Harold Macmillan who began to appear as the apostle of peace. He went to Moscow and prepared for the Summit in Paris in May 1960, which was ruined by the spy flight of the American U2, inopportunely brought down by the Russians!

A group of us women, representing the Caravan of Peace, lobbied the Embassies in Paris with an appeal. We were well received though not at top level: I recall the sight of Macmillan's anxious face as he drove by, near to the British

Embassy.

In the intervening twenty years, except that the situation has acquired a greater urgency and terror, nothing has changed since I wrote that last chapter, from which I quote this paragraph:

> The Peace and Nuclear Disarmament Movements of East and West are hoist with their own petard, in that they have been content to remain prisoners of their respective ideologies, and, since both remain actuated by ulterior motives, they have not, any more than the statesmen, really abandoned the chess board moves of power politics and faced the problem of laying the foundation of a world disarmed. For that foundation lies in the end to the cold war and to the propaganda of hate and suspicion which alone maintain it and alone make possible the bogy of the 'balance of terror'. The peoples of the world, so said President Eisenhower in one of his better moods, desire peace so much that they will presently push the statesmen aside if they do not get it.

Had this been true in word and deed, the Summit of May 1960 could not have failed.

The attempt of the Helsinki agreements has failed for similar reasons. Each sectional group of human beings is always trying to 'get under the other fellow's skin'.

We do now begin to understand that any war to-day is total war. To this the only answer is total peace. This does not mean that we must have an oppressive World Government under which everyone must think, believe and act alike. It means only that we must learn to accept that, though our planet is small, it will always contain peoples of infinite variety of religious and political beliefs and customs.

It has also, so far, been the home of innumerable species of animals and plants; great beauties of unsullied landscape — waters, seas, light and air. All this we can love and cherish or destroy.

We have the mind, imagination and skill to do either. The choice is ours.

Part Eight

IN A MAN'S WORLD: THE ECLIPSE OF WOMAN

1965

Before the modern women's movement made its presence widely felt, Dora Russell was stating the case – which almost two decades later remains just as relevant.

IN A MAN'S WORLD:
THE ECLIPSE OF WOMAN

Mrs. Pankhurst's statue stands hard by the Houses of Parliament and, not long since, an addition to the statue commemorated her daughter Christabel. Very large numbers of people in Great Britain assume, when they think of the matter at all, that the battle of women for equal rights with men has long since been won. A closer look at the present day status of women, however, makes one wonder whether there is a real basis for this optimistic assumption. The recent publication by the National Council for Civil Liberties of its pamphlet on the disabilities under which women still suffer will reinforce such misgivings.

To detail the manifold information of this pamphlet here would be inappropriate. What concerns me here is not so much the victories of varying importance still waiting to be won, as the question, to me the most important of all, as to how far women are able to influence the shape and trend of society as a whole. Many women, of course, especially in political life in this country, deny that any special stress should be laid on a woman's point of view. It is interesting to note that this attitude is in marked contrast to that obtaining in countries where women reached equality recently as part of a general revolution. In such countries one finds that women form themselves into huge united organisations, who take it for granted that they are there to speak 'as women', while the ratio of women to men in their national assemblies is higher than in our own Parliament.

In Italy the vote came to women after World War II: one of the first tasks of the developing women's movement was to care for the families left destitute and maimed by the war, hence they have always combined a strong maternal attitude with their feminism. In India the great Women's Congresses are more influential than such gatherings in Britain. While, even in a small country like Albania, women now enjoy great prestige and their public work is held in high esteem. They are in fact given some preference over men for some superior positions.

In Britain in almost any office or Civil Service department one will find women to a large extent employed on the more mechanical work, or – if in the upper grades – acting as lieutenant, right hand, or 'office wife' to the man at the top. Nor is this because the women lack the ability to become top executives or administrators; on the contrary, often it is their very ability as second in command that bolsters up the position of their chief. Possibly women lack the bounce and self-confidence to take on responsibility, but this is largely due to their education and the general estimate of them as 'second class' citizens. Milton's 'He for God only, she for God in him' has sunk deep into our social and economic pattern. Yet take a look at women in those spheres recognised by tradition as peculiarly theirs – as midwives, mothers, chancellor of the exchequer in the home – here is no lack of initiative or shouldering of responsibility.

The education of women requires our attention, the more so as it was the subject not long since of a controversy sparked off by Sir John Newsom in the *Observer*. It was argued, among other points, that an academic, over-rational, theoretical type of learning was unsuited to women, that it also unfitted them for the more concrete and instinctive occupations of maternity and child care. The male contributions to the discussion were remarkable in illustrating how great a degree of prejudice still exists in Western countries against women of high intelligence and learning, of which there is further proof in the very small percentage of women able to get to the Universities, to study medicine, or to reach the top posts in any intellectual profession. Nor did it seem to occur to anyone that this prejudice – and many other signs – indicates that there is something very wrong with the education of *men*, whose curriculum and mental attitudes are obsolete and little adapted to the world in which they have to live to-day.

To take a small example: the first secondary schools for girls, founded by the Girls' Public Day School Trust, were not obliged to struggle against the stranglehold of the Classics on education. For the most part, their pupils concentrated on modern languages and the sciences, cramming Latin and Greek only when these were required for admission to a University. But the persistence of classical education for men of our upper classes has been a powerful and in many respects adverse influence on educational advance as on our political and economic life. While not decrying the enriching of our imagination and language by classical studies, one cannot help reflecting on the countless small boys construing the exploits of the Roman legions in Gaul and Britain, and seeing themselves as the Caesars of the future, conquering 'regions Caesar never knew, over which their posterity has held sway' – that is, until this day and age. Greek rationalism and mathematics have, however, been a most potent influence on the evolution of our present day society.

Such is the fear of women that it has been, by tradition, essential to a man's education that he should, from an early age, be removed from feminine influence – sons were taken from their mothers to begin a process of hardening for knighthood, or to go to the monastery for learning; at a later date we find the young boy hustled off to prep school; while, only the other day, I read a statement by a headmaster that all children should spend some time at boarding school, to get them away from their mothers.

In so far as education for women was considered at all, men's first notions appear to have been that it should not only differ from that of men, but should, in all respects, be related to men's needs.

Not to elaborate on the notions of feminine personality that have prevailed down the ages, let us quote from the *Sermons for Young Women* of Dr. Fordyce, much read when Mary Wollstonecraft was preparing to write her *Vindication of the Rights of Women* in the eighteenth century. Women, according to Dr. Fordyce, should be 'meek, timid, yielding, complacent, sweet, benign and tender'; their propensity to 'melt into affectionate sorrow' is their great charm; while 'war, commerce, exercises of strength and dexterity, abstract philosophy and all the abstruser sciences are not for women'. And many must be familiar with Rousseau's notion of the functions of women: 'to please, to be useful to us, to make us love and esteem them, to educate us when young and take care of us when grown up, to advise, to console us, to render our lives easy and agreeable: these are the duties of women at all times and what they should be taught in their infancy'.

Before relegating this thesis to the antique past, let us reflect for one moment on the type of activity and morals inculcated week by week in the women of to-day by the women's magazines with their five and six million circulation – a most potent educational influence on the younger generation. Is their point of view so very different from that of Rousseau, or the Rev. Dr. Fordyce?

At the same time compare the many aids to beauty and hints on sex appeal contained in these journals with the terms of the Act passed by our Parliament in 1770, which laid down that 'all women of whatever age, rank or profession or degree, whether virgin, maid or widow that shall from and after such Act impose upon, seduce or betray into matrimony any of His Majesty's subjects, by means of scent, paints, cosmetics, washes, artificial teeth, false hair, Spanish wool, iron stays, hoops, high heeled shoes or bolstered hips shall incur the penalty of the law now in force against witchcraft and like misdemeanours, and that the marriage upon conviction shall stand null and void.' I wonder if this Act has ever been repealed – and how devastating might be its effect nowadays!

The early feminists can scarcely be blamed for seeking to prove that women could learn and do all that became a man – after all, it is a man's world in which women have to live. Nor, even if it were desirable, is there much scope in present day society for sex differences in education. We live in a utilitarian state, in which the chief value of the individual is measured by the service or the function which he or she performs. Our educational factories, year by year, must turn out a sufficient production quota of civil servants, doctors, dentists, lawyers, managers, advertising agents, technologists, scientists, teachers, skilled workers and efficient instruments in the supply of goods and services.

Obviously, practically every one of these jobs can be equally well performed by a man or a woman; at least, this is the assumption on which, allowing for certain discriminations against women which still exist, our organisation as a community is based. We further require of these units in our society that they should be sufficiently disciplined to go to work at stated times, to work stated hours, and, on the whole, to remain in the chosen occupation most or all of their working life. To endure this discipline, which is an integral requirement of industrial civilisation, the individual must acquire and hold a belief in the ultimate aims and purposes to which the elaborate machine, of which he is a small part, is directed. These aims are, in fact, called in question by many individuals and groups at the present time: this is one reason for the frustration which undoubtedly exists, especially among women and young people. To this point we will return later.

Thus increasing stress is laid nowadays on vocational education, a fact sometimes deplored by the administrators of Universities in which the ancient traditions of learning and research for their own sake still survive. But, since training for a function, in a highly organised society, becomes steadily more essential and complex, it begins to take up more time and to dwarf all other considerations and educational needs.

Now it is a serious error either for the individual or for society as a whole to make the 'work function' the central point and focus of life and education. For in performing, however well, a function for which an individual has been trained, he or she is not necessarily acting as a complete human being. Moreover, stressing work function unduly, we begin to think of people as neuters, or even as automata.

What I wish to emphasise most strongly here is that 'work function' is only a small part of an individual. A human being has many other functions, as citizen, husband or wife, father or mother, thinker or dreamer. Both in education and in life we tend to split the human personality into these separate compartments, making it difficult for the man or woman to express himself or herself as a whole. We separate work from enjoyment, home from the outside world, imply a conflict between marriage and a career.

Of late I have been much struck by the frequent assumption that marriage and parenthood are a sort of trap, the virtual end of a woman, as well as of a man, as a freely developing individual. Surely to fall in love, to have children, should represent a new and wonderful stage in the unfolding of a human personality; it is tragic to envelop this with a sense of resentment and unwilling personal sacrifice.

Does this attitude arise because individuals have come to believe that their roles in society as a whole are also those most important to themselves? Is this an acceptance of the values of society or the State then, and, if so, what are these values?

The dilemma of the split between the more or less impersonal life of the job and the personal life of home is one which, in the present state of opinion and social organisation, bears most hardly on women. To suggest that they should be educated mainly for maternal functions is patently absurd, when one realises that for most of them the choice between marriage and a career no longer exists. One third of the labour force which keeps our economy going and contributes to our wealth is composed of women. Of these about one half now are married. In the near future it is likely that the proportion of married women gainfully employed will rise still further, firstly because the sexes are now more evenly balanced in numbers and secondly because both men and women are marrying and starting their families much younger than in the days of their parents and grandparents.

Since our society cannot now, apparently, do without the contribution made by women's work and there is no pool of life-long spinsters on which to draw, we are faced with the necessity of making it possible for mothers to work outside the home without harmful results to their children or too great a drain on their own energy and health. The confusion that exists in the minds of our administrators about this far from simple problem is shown by the frenzied appeals of the Ministry of Education to married women teachers to return to work, coupled with the absolute refusal of local authorities to carry out the terms of the 1944 Education Act, which expressly laid down the provision of nursery schools.

Some social scientists have been marking out a nice, neat pattern for the life of a woman in the future, according to which she will do some kind of work after leaving school, University or Training College. She will then spend a period having two or three children, returning to work – after some re-training – when these are of school age. The drawback to this plan is that, like part-time work, it means that women will inevitably do the less skilled tasks and will be looked upon as a pool of labour to fill in gaps as required. To pursue a profession or skilled job continuously and to be valued for this as an individual will scarcely be possible in these circumstances.

There is really no other way of solving the problem of a mother at work with benefit to her as well as the children than by the provision of nursery schools, clubs and play centres suited to different ages. Frequent objection is made that family life is broken up if each member, from an early age, starts to go his or her own way, to the neglect of the ties which should bind them to father and mother, brothers and sisters. Above all, mother should be there for the young ones, who will suffer greatly if they lack the security and warmth of her care in early years, whilst the older children will become delinquent or disgruntled if they cannot come back from school to the cosiness of a home and a mother receptive to their confidences.

To me these arguments do seem to have some validity, but they lie oddly in the mouths of many of those who advance them. For these objectors are, by and large, those very persons in government and industry who create the social and economic system which presents mothers with this dilemma.

When one looks at the whole background, physical, social, economic, of the modern biological family, the remarkable thing is that it manages to survive at all. To begin with, what social researchers somewhat unfortunately call the 'nuclear' family, consisting of mother, father and two or three children living in their separate little box of a flat or house, is quite a new development. Previously the family was much more of a clan, in which children grew up in close association with grandparents, many aunts, uncles and cousins. Studies in the East End have shown how tenacious these relationships are when married couples live either with or near the older generation. Mothers and daughters still shop and housekeep almost jointly and see each other four or five times a week. Village life, until the younger people began to move away to the towns, allowed of an even closer attachment between the generations. Sometimes this could be excessive, in that elderly sons and daughters remained at home with a still child-like attitude to their aging, surviving parent. In the larger towns nowadays, planning, which plants the small family units out into new towns or housing estates, leaves behind the Grans and Granpas either in the sad, dilapidated old premises, or else perched up in one of the modern blocks with their dizzy gangways.

Once more we observe the increasing tendency for each individual to live a separate existence, depending on the State and community for the care and service previously rendered by the family. Apart from breakfast and week-end meals families no longer often eat together; the home is empty all day except for the mother and the youngest children, unless she also goes out to work. It is not surprising that mothers have recently been complaining of loneliness and isolation from the life of the community, or that many of them go out to work as soon as possible for the sake of companionship with other women and a sense of 'belonging'.

That ideal home with the fridge and washing machine and streamlined kitchen – as advertised by the women's magazines – is seen to be a hollow sham. A snare, too, is the 'women's world apart' in which these journals perpetuate, for adult women, the fairy tale world of childhood in which princess meets prince and lives happy ever after. To the opium administered by the women's magazines can be attributed to a large extent the apathy of younger women to-day as regards certain of their interests, and the ineffectiveness of women in the political world.

But if the home now lacks former human warmth, the outside world is no better. Take political life: I have never been able to understand why we should have wanted women in politics, if not because they are women and not men. But the politician and the career woman do not agree with this. In politics, a sexless citizen functionary in each of us is deemed to exercise its judgment between the varying programmes presented to the voter. In fact, as we all know, rational choice is possibly the last factor influencing the average voter: prejudices, sex differences, confused emotions of all kinds play their part. And political women more and more deny that Parliament is anything but a career for them as for men; they toe the Party line more assiduously than their male colleagues; they argue that, because they represent all their constituents, therefore special championship of women's causes is out of place. This assumption works very well in maintaining the dominance of male values, but one does not notice that Trade Union members or company directors in Parliament fail, directly or indirectly, to support their own interests. And never was the male viewpoint on sex more blatant in politics than in the debates not long since on the iniquitous Street Offences Bill, which, in our attitude to prostitutes, set us back to the time before Josephine Butler's magnificent crusade on their behalf. Another example, this time of women expressing their specific view on a sex question, is the campaign in the 1920's by the Labour women to get advice on family limitation accepted as right and proper and given as an integral part of maternity care. This campaign raised an outcry against women for 'dragging sex into politics'. Their aim is not yet fully achieved in this country, although the population question is now crucial for our overcrowded island and for world policies.

Are not, however, individuals far more independent in these days, and have they not, in consequence, greater freedom in discussion of sex matters and in their sexual behaviour? It is perfectly true that freedom from taboos is important, as is the decline in the double standard of morality as between men and women. Social and religious teachers have frequently insisted on love for our fellow creatures as the basic factor in social cohesion. Love is not primarily of the spirit; it flows from the biological sanctions of sex and parental feeling. It can be sublimated or extended into love for the children of others, for our own people, for the whole human race. But such extension will not take place if society ceases to value the personal sources of this love, between young lovers, husbands and wives, members of a family, the young for the old. Where the lonely individual has to make his way and come to terms with the juggernaut of large scale organisation, love will count for little and devil take the hindmost will be the motto.

It seems to me that nowadays we have a very great deal more sex, with little increase, even, it may be, a decrease, in the volume of love. Women are so eager to emulate men that they have carried this aspiration even into the sexual sphere, approximating to men in their sex relations and taking sex, as do numbers of men, as the satisfaction of a purely physical appetite. I would not wish women to pretend, as the Victorians tried to do, that physical sex enjoyment does not exist for women, nor would I wish to give the impression of condemning casual sex encounters. But, if we are to speak of *love*, this also does not exist without some mutual feeling for and understanding of each other's personality. And women could do more to make men understand that the question 'do you really love me?' is not without meaning.

The emphasis on sex, as opposed to parenthood, is yet another example of the dominance of male concepts. For men, biologically speaking, sex and procreation are one and the same act. For women the two exist quite distinct from one another. The moment of sexual pleasure is one thing: the emotional and actual experience of the long period of pregnancy quite another. It seems strange that women have not given more attention to the psychological, economic and social consequences of this difference. Much of their political weakness flows from their failure to make those demands on society that their maternal role requires. In their enthusiasm for conquering men's world, they failed to defend the world that was their own. Not only that, but in their early political struggles, they joined with men in giving a low status to the bearing and rearing of children and concern with domestic life.

The reaction, described by Betty Friedan in *The Feminine Mystique*, which has led women to deny their own intelligence and education and retreat into the role of housewife and mother, is equally mistaken. It is not solely in the home and in one family, that children need to be nurtured and defended. A thousand and one demands in their name have to be made on our affluent and bellicose society and its myopic planners.

Stress on the sex act, with all the glamour with which the advertising world surrounds it for the adolescent, intensifies the narcissism which is not unnatural at that stage of development. Women become preoccupied with aids to eternal youth and beauty, young men aspire to be pop singers, to show off on motor bikes, to despise girls, to shun the trap of marriage and to find in homosexual relations not only a natural expression of sex at that age, but also a convenient way of avoiding unwanted babies. On the whole it is the male 'image' that prevails. Those who are old enough to remember the vogue of the 'Gaiety girls' and the plump pantomime 'boys' will note that the most admired performer in the variety world to-day is the slim young male. When women appear, on the whole, in figure and dress, they emulate the male idol. In spite of all the 'free love', there is little balance and harmony here between the sexes. Balance and harmony presupposes the recognition of differences to be brought together, whereas it is the fallacy of thinking that equality is the same as being identical which prevails.

And when we talk of free love how often do we reflect that this whole concept is negated by the offer of sex for sale? Women can still sell their sex in the hope of a lifelong meal-ticket from a well-to-do husband, or in successive marriages and divorces, to grow affluent on alimony; prostitution is on the increase; gigolos seek rich women patrons, homosexuals patrons of their own sex.

Recently there has been much discussion about the increase of illegitimate children. These are not only born to so-called ignorant and innocent girls, they appear at all levels of society and some are born to women who, in the view of the stern moralist, are old enough to know better. An encouraging feature of this state of affairs is that the stern moralist is no longer setting the pace. Neither those who help the unmarried mother nor she herself is inclined to accept her predicament as shameful. But her economic dilemma, side by side with that of the deserted wife or the widow with young children, is bringing women up sharply against the diminished sense of responsibility of men for the children they have begotten whether in or out of wedlock. In a fairly recent debate on widows' pensions, Mr. Douglas Houghton, M.P., expressed his surprise that, in the changing and dangerous world in which we live, women should still commit the economic support of themselves and their children to their marriage lines. The many anomalies about widows' pensions go to show the absurdity of hanging the support of a woman with children, or an elderly woman who has spent her life in domesticity, simply on the fact of her legal marriage and its duration. What mothers need help and money and pensions for is the – at present unpaid – work which they do in the home, which is a service to society and not only to the husband, however stable the marriage. Moreover a long period of marriage ending in divorce deprives the wife of the ultimate status of widow. It is not surprising that men, who are aware of what the State will now do for their children and the fact that their wives can earn, do show less economic responsibility and respect for the marriage tie. Neither are wives exempt from this accusation. But in fact, though there may be many husbands who share common family duties, the wife, having lost her pre-industrial status as the centre of the family, finds more and more burdens heaped upon her. She earns for her children, keeps and decorates the family home, cooks, cleans, mends for husband and children, hunts for a place to live, helps to drive and clean the family car, if it exists. And week by week is subjected to a blast of propaganda urging her never to look outside the walls of her home.

What really does happen to the children? Are they really loved? Many of them are deprived of one parent or the other, by divorce if not by death, a shocking number of them are taken into the care of local authorities on account of the cruelty and neglect of their parents, or the fact that society itself is so neglectful that their whole family has no home to live in. The discovery that the beating up of young babies by their parents is not uncommon has recently shocked doctors and the public. Whether we like it or not, the only solution for all this confusion is that the community should take full responsibility for seeing that women with young children, whether wives, widows or unmarried, should have all the support and help that will be needed for the children to fulfil themselves as human beings and as citizens. So long as the machine age continues, it is not possible to return to the old style system, though we should still try to see that education and living conditions foster and keep alive family ties. Let those who do enjoy the comforts of family life reflect on the meaning for children of those cases quite often reported in the Press when brothers and sisters taken 'into care' vanish into separate institutions and may never find each other again so long as they live.

So far, then, the education and emancipation of women would seem to have done little more, in our own country, than fit women more neatly into the existing structure of industrial society, a society which would also appear, from the foregoing, to be inimical to their deepest interests and needs. The present state of the world is the measure, not of women's success, but rather of their failure. What do they get for all the work and services that they perform? To what extent, for instance, does our State carry out those projects which women consider important? Do women agree that vast sums be spent for nuclear arms, space rockets and war, while biology, medicine, the social sciences and education are starved? Ought not women to make themselves heard on such vital top-level decisions?

To me it has always seemed that the challenge which faces women in the modern world is something much deeper than the struggle for political or economic rights. We have been discussing here the inroads of the State into our private lives with, as must be admitted, some benefit to the people. But what in effect is this State, on which we tend to rely more and more to play father and mother to its citizens? It is mechanical, bureaucratic, power-loving, sadistic, war-like, repressive. By its very nature, history and principles, it cannot deal constructively with human problems. It is founded on the principle of keeping order by force within the State and by force giving battle to enemies without. In accord with this concept, for instance, it seeks to deal with crime and juvenile delinquency by a great increase in the pay of the police, while insulting and underpaying the teaching and nursing profession. The tragedy of its traditional attitude in foreign affairs needs no emphasis.

Ultimately it is with this encroaching industrial State machine that women have been engaged in battle ever since they first sought emancipation. At first confused, they made for the vote. But events have made them aware that unless they emerge from their streamlined or dingy kitchens to demand much more, not only their families but all humanity may stand in great peril.

The clue to Mrs. Pankhurst's crusade lies in a paragraph on the first page of the book *Unshackled* by her daughter Christabel.

> The industrial North is an effectual school of politics and economics, and Mother fully learnt its lesson. The seamy side of industrialism and the manifold need of reform appear there in reality. Smoke-darkened skies, a mixture of smoke and air to breathe, the blotting out of Nature's green life, colourless streets, mean and even insanitary housing, mechanical noise, the monotonous yet precarious toil of wage-earners, the premature tearing from school and play of children, the anxious life of mothers, too scantily fed to bear strong babies, too poor to feed them properly as they grew – these and other plagues were rampant in Lancashire when Mother's days began.

The more sordid features of industrialism may have begun at long last to disappear, but the rigid and close knit organisation on which it depends has become ever more intense, as well as the extreme discipline of mind and body without which the operation of modern devices is impossible. It has become the enemy of all that is spontaneous and anarchic in biological life, those impulses that specifically matter to women. It surprised me that no reviewer remarked on the underlying message of Dürrenmatt's play, *The Physicists*, in which the ridiculing of the wife and sons and the strangling of the nurses was symbolical of women's irrelevance. The final triumph in the play fell to the woman scientist – a crippled travesty of her sex – who imitated men's evil drive to power by the misuse of science.

Fundamentally, men have always loved themselves and their purposes better than they have loved women. There was a time when superstition enveloped agriculture, fertility was worshipped and there was a cult of goddesses. But as men began to work in metals, to acquire knowledge and skills, superstition declined and patriarchal power began to come into its own. To-day fertility may well be looked upon as a curse rather than a blessing, and therefore imparts no prestige to being a woman.

In a recent book Robert Graves wrote as follows: 'In my view the political and social confusion of these last 3,000 years has been entirely due to man's revolt against woman as a priestess of natural magic, and his defeat of her wisdom by the use of intellect.' This is of special interest taken side by side with the remarks of Martin James, a psychiatrist, in the Newsom controversy. He is insufferably condescending. 'Many Englishmen of the boarding school class . . . have to relearn from their wives that people can be childish and irrational and are, in fact, *human*; they have been taught to idealise pure logic and reason, often at the expense of emotion. Such husbands serve as yet another unplanned influence which reinforces the ideal of rationality for the woman parent and undermines her child-centred assumptions.'

And again: 'Women's apparent illogicality is really a devious logic which is a delight both to themselves and their men. It is in fact just as consecutive and sensible in its own way as conceptual rationality based on secondary process and secondary education.' (So complacent is Martin James in his conviction that his male 'ideal of rationality' must predominate, that it does not even occur to him that, in this instance, it is the masculine education which is misdirected.)

George Meredith is wiser:

Their sense is with their senses all mixed in
Destroyed by subtleties these women are
More brain, O Lord, more brain, or we shall mar
Utterly this fair garden we might win.

And the Chinese writer Han Suyin:

O what a fool is man, who clutches at the firmament, forgetting that the earth is a star. . . .

I am earth-bound and so remain. I am a woman, obdurate, rooted, clinging to sight and smell and feel, suspicious of abstractions.

What is being said here in various ways is important and significant.

When men first began to use reason, to study mathematics and the universe about them, they found in this an escape from servitude to their biological existence, even, by means of god and religion, the hope of escape from individual death. Women, because of men's sexual needs, were always associated with the animal side of men's natures. In between moments of sexual excitement women did not exist for men, who then felt themselves the cool, rational, spiritual beings which they aspired to become.

And Robert Graves is so right: on this worship of the intellect, on this escapism, on this split between mind and matter, body and soul, men have built their philosophies, their concepts of government, their States, down the ages. With Newton and Cartesian man – 'give me matter and motion and I will construct the world' – 'reason the charioteer of the passions' – come the notions of the 'clockwork universe' and 'man's conquest of nature' on which ultimately the industrial states are built.

Power was always the concept on which man based the authority of the State, first the authority of the tyrant, or the divine right of the king, but latterly the worship of mechanism and the thrust of dynamic power. A relic of the old concept is to have a dictator – or old man of the tribe – at the top.

Everything must proceed in tidiness and order. Curves abound in nature – as in women – but in the main curves are 'out' so far as architects and planners are concerned. Roads must be wide and straight for the worshipped car, to whose death-dealing propensities there is an astounding indifference. In place of the cathedrals we now have the glass and concrete skyscrapers – symbol, as one of their architects himself recently put it – of virility. The rocket, fed by fire and thrusting into space, is the most perfect phallic symbol of all, except that its warhead carries death instead of the seeds of life. Perhaps that, too, is significant.

To halt this race towards suicide, a new concept of the State and human purpose is required. It is one that will never be achieved by men alone. Women's views must not be brushed aside as of no importance; women must be encouraged to speak and to use that wisdom which they undoubtedly possess, however much overlaid it has become by masculine ascendancy. Women are not by nature escapists, they are, on the whole, at home in the natural world. Giving birth, they do literally create 'in the flesh' and there is nothing in animal life that they would despise unless taught – as they have been – to do so. Already the emphasis on natural childbirth is a fresh assertion of women's dignity. Moreover the bearing and rearing of children has become endowed with a new significance by advances of medicine, psychology, psychiatry and education. Women are aware that parenthood and all those activities that rest upon it, medical care, the schools, the social services, are far more important than training more technologists for industry.

We have begun to understand that we do, in fact, by heredity and environment, create human beings who tend to carry forward the patterns which we set them, and who are, in very truth, the future of our race. This idea, which brought with it the concept of 'child-centred' education, is relatively new in our world. It means that we can play a more conscious part in the evolution of humanity.

However much we may admire the achievements of man in science – and no woman would be so ungenerous as to deny them – women do know that man in his intoxication with mechanism and industrial production may well be nearing a dead end. If we are to make possible further achievements of the human spirit, then we need new people rather than new machines.

Somehow we have to make an end of what Robert Graves so aptly calls the rule of 'mechanarchy'. It is necessary to reconcile industrial man with his older environment – the world of plants and animals, the world of life and growth, which measures time, not by clocks, but by darkness and the dawn, the weather and the seasons. Man has to learn to curb his restless search for power, learn to live in peace with his fellow men, to stop raping and squandering the resources of our planet for profit and greed.

It is the education of *men* rather than that of women which needs to become more concrete and personal, to deal less in abstractions, theories, and general rational concepts.

Women's achievements have shown that they are well able to cope with an education determined by men, what they look for now is that men's education should move in their direction. Men have made at least one step forward by beginning to resolve the dualism of mind and matter.

Education, our pundits still tell us, must produce more top ranking people trained in science, so that we may be able to compete with our industrial rivals overseas. What nonsense all this is. Is industry to go on expanding and expanding, like the porridge pot in the fairy tale, till it floods all and no one can stop it? Already a large new industry is growing up in the United States for destroying industrial products, so that more may be sold and more profit made.

We have to begin educating boys and girls to be human beings, instead of drilling them in 'subjects' for exams and the rat race of a career. They need wider views, not so much narrow specialisation, they need to be able to look at their world as a whole.

At present aggression and competitiveness are still fostered, disobedience to arbitrary authority is still visited with the violence of the cane. Yet much research has shown that these methods induce bad behaviour rather than conformity. Other experiments have shown that it is possible to educate children for democracy, tolerance and co-operation, by measures of self-government, helped by adults who guide but do not stand constantly on their dignity.

Above all it is education for living and human relations which should be uppermost. Both boys and girls need to learn that, whatever fun one may have with sex, its most lovely use is as an instrument of sensitive and subtle understanding. Parenthood should be presented, not as self-satisfaction and self-aggrandizement, but as the most important activity on which both men and women can be engaged. If this were accepted, there would be immense changes in the organisation and direction of our economic and social life.

Rational man, industrial man, man the scientist, man

the escapist, sets his sights for a landing on the moon. Meantime he murders and prepares to murder millions of his own kind and ignores other countless millions who are ignorant, starving and diseased. Is it for this that we should live and that women should bear children?

Only by valuing life and creation and by seeing in the nurture of our children the possibilities of our future shall we be able so to shape the purposes of the State that it turns from violence, greed and inhuman planning, to become the true father and mother of the people. Man and woman, neither dominant, working together, could achieve this. So far as we know, such a thing has never yet happened in human history. To see it come to pass is the hope of many young people, both men and women, of this generation.

Are they, too, crying for the moon?

Part Nine

THINKING ABOUT TIME

1969

Inextricably woven through her understandings about male consciousness, the machine age, and domination and exploitation, are Dora Russell's reflections upon the way we have structured *time* in our society. The following article helps to summarise her view.

THINKING ABOUT TIME

As I look out of my window and watch the majestic march of great clouds across the sky, the wheeling of the gulls, the sweep of the wind over bushes and grass; or as I sit on the fine turf, scented with wild thyme, of a granite cliff top, high above a restless sea – amid all this movement and change I get a sense of infinity, permanence and peace.

In the days when I had to live and work in London, my source of relaxation was to board a night train for Cornwall, to fall asleep on the wide, cheap, simple berths we had in those days, and to wake to a world in which the noise and fret of the city had vanished, a world of rain and shine and – timelessness.

Now rarely in these days does anyone speak, or even think, about eternity. Yet in the days before men began to measure time, it must have seemed to them that they lived in that state, with mysterious changes of light and dark, or weather and seasons, a strange world of magic, none of it to be measured in time or catalogued into compartments, bounded only by the greatest mystery – death. In a mood of timelessness one cannot help but understand how much they must have longed to find out how to live forever, how deeply they were attached to a changeless existence: 'as it was in the beginning, is now and ever shall be, world without end, Amen.'

Of course, the period of profound Christian belief never loses sight of eternity, of eternal bliss or eternal damnation.

To Andrew Marvell in his great poem, Time was a wingéd chariot hurrying between 'deserts of vast eternity'. Milton challenged the destructiveness of Time: 'Fly, envious Time, till thou run out thy race' but ended with the glory of life eternal:

> Attired like stars, we shall forever sit
> Triumphing over Death and Chance, and Thee, O Time.

How significant is that coupling of chance with death, expressing man's constant search for order and security.

The ancient astronomers calculated the years by the stars, and the finger of the Sun, great Lord of all, wrote the hours in shadows on the dials; sand falling in the hourglass, the tallow candle, the water clock, all these mankind, anxiously aware of their short span of life, made use of to measure its passing.

With the measurement of time by means of a machine made in metal by man, there comes a whole new era. Simple natural materials are left behind and a new word – clockwork – comes into our vocabulary. We speak of clockwork precision, clockwork efficiency. The planets are seen to revolve according to mathematical laws; the God who created them is called by many of his worhsippers the Great Clockmaker of the Universe. Was not man himself, perhaps, merely a machine? his destiny unalterable in the vast mechanism of the universal clock? From this date on, it seems to me, the concept of time has never been dissociated in the Western mind from that of machinery.

Measuring time we become conscious of the past, the present and the future. Historians record our past, much of our present is spent in planning, prophesying; dreaming of future bliss, or dreading future disaster. The foresight that comes of the time sense is valuable, as our unrelenting researches into our origins and the sources of life.

But time seems to lose its old static quality: it becomes an 'ever-rolling stream', a conveyor belt on which things move in a linear direction, now fast, now slow, but always – and here comes that fatal word now almost invariably linked with time – always with 'progress.' Since we have evolved from more primitive beginnings, then indeed every move onwards, so we believe, must be an advance – in civilisation, skills, knowledge, what you will. The mere concept of time spells progress. Things will always be better to-morrow than they were yesterday or to-day.

So the great adventure with Time begins. We calculate time scientifically, and map our world with lines to facilitate commerce and navigation. More and more we remove ourselves from the time of our agricultural period, we live, eat and drink, work, sleep and travel by the clock. 'There's no time to waste; it's not time for that; Time, gentlemen, please', we cry. At the factory, day or night, we clock in and clock out. Subdividing time becomes an exquisite art in manufacture; it invades also our leisure entertainments – thus radio and television programmes are timed to the minute and even less. And then there is speed. How splendid it is to defeat Time by ever faster travel, first the stage coach, then rail, and now automobile and supersonic flight. No more of Milton's 'lazy leaden-stepping hours' for us.

Since we live by the clocks, nothing is simpler than to change them. Of course we did set them as scientifically as possible by the sun in the first place, reckoning that at midday the sun would be directly over our heads. But, if it be more convenient for us all to arrange to have more daylight in summer, or in winter to grope our way to work in extra dark (so that the tycoons who rule us and who live by light artificial may defeat time in their business communications) – why then simply turn the clock hands round. How comes it in this technological age that such departures from one of the basic events of our planet – the rising and setting of the sun – should be so lightly disregarded by our men of science? Thus it was with some satisfaction that I observed that the transfer from capsule to ship of the first men to return from the moon had to be delayed until such *time* as the rising of the sun should permit television to show this final triumph to the world.

Only those who understand the calculations can really grasp the meaning of Einstein's space-time. But shifts in concepts and emphasis by the mind and imagination of mankind seem to take place, as it were, all in one piece. So that ordinary men and women, not in the least understanding Einstein, suddenly find themselves weary of a clockwork world of dynamics and the unending 'march of time'. 'Stop the World, I want to get off' is a quip that expresses well the increasing boredom of men and women with time and motion study and exhortations to ever greater productivity and efficiency. The well regulated universe of the Great Clockmaker and his prophet Isaac Newton, together with man's own attempt to imitate its plan in the shaping of his own society, suddenly seem like a prison.

Researches into the mind and nature of man himself have indicated a way of escape. However marvellous it may seem to fly so fast as to arrive before you start, this involves a contraption with hundreds of dials and gadgets, and the labour and scientific application of thousands of human beings. Whereas the mind and imagination of one man alone can, in a split second, project itself far into his past; can, in present time, withdraw into a world of his own, there to imagine and thus, perhaps, shape his future. There is, it seems, a timeless time, in which we can live concurrently with that of the old conveyor belt. This is, perhaps, our only experience of eternity.

The shift taking place in the modern mood is leading to further exploration of the potential of the timeless world of memory and imagination. Possibly there is nothing new in this. It may be no more than a throwback to those ages before intellect, reason, calculation and the quantitative method of science took so firm a hold on the mental, moral, physical and economic structure of our lives.

Those to whom the timeless world may seem more real than what is called reality are stigmatised by practical men as mere idealists and dreamers. But how has anything in the 'real' man-made world come about except through shapes foreshadowed in man's dreams? If we are determined by the tools we use, or our 'means of production', this is merely because we will it so. 'We are such stuff as dreams are made on –'.

It is no mere accident that the arts, and especially poetry, have lately shown such fresh vitality. In a world dominated by time and change men seem always to have found in art some glimpse of eternity.

Tout passe
Tout lasse
L'art robuste

Seul a l'éternité.

So must the builders of the great cathedrals and Michel Angelo have felt, as they laboured for posterity. So, too, the men of the eighteenth century, as they laid out their parks and planted their trees.

The creation of language, its gradual development, the skill and beauty of its use is as subtle and remarkable an invention as any of the mechanical or electronic age. Consider too, how a composer may hold within himself the intricate music of an entire symphony, writing it down, it may be, without even playing a note. We are very far from understanding how our bodies put forth creative efforts. For surely such creation resides not only in the brain; think, for instance of the perfect rhythm of the skater or dancer. It may well be that the body has its own rhythms and time sense closely allied to the virtually unalterable rhythms of our revolving planet. Could these not perhaps be in conflict with the speed and time by which at present we have set our travel and periods of work? Does the human organism really function as it should when hurled at a great height and speed through space to take some vital decision which may affect the lives of millions? What really are the long term effects of running factories round the clock in shifts both night and day?

That there are problems here is shown by the studies now being made of what may happen when a man is isolated from all contact with time and the daily round for some considerable period; or when an attempt is made to 'set' men to a twenty-seven hour clock. The relation of dreams to the depth of sleep; of dreams and thought to the patterns made by the waves of the brain are also the subject of intensive research. And what is the meaning of the almost manic need of our age for constant background music? and the growing tendency to escape into hallucination by drugs? What, deep down, is the meaning of the student revolt?

It may well be that, as we become more interested in the inner life of human beings, the extrovert pleasure of 'conquering Nature' and of possessing an ever greater variety of the consumer goods offered by the machine, will give way to more contemplative forms of enjoyment. As we find that we desire less, we may manufacture less, and gradually tone down our production to our basic needs.

So we might set ourselves free from clockwork time, free once more to pursue learning, art and wisdom for their own sake; free to look upon the beauty of a landscape without an urge to 'develop' it, or upon a garden and not turn it into a car park. We could even be free of the tyranny of the motor car, of the restless discontent that keeps us ever on the move; free to deal with the ugliness we have made in our own land instead of seeking beauty in others; free to live not as predators, but as fellow creatures, with the infinite variety of non-human life in the world; free to do nothing but be glad to be alive, and to give to 'progress' a totally different meaning from that which it has borne for three hundred years, while dominated by a misguided use of the discoveries of science.

Hopes such as these do not easily arise in minds imprisoned in our spreading urban network. Against the natural forces of wind, weather and the seasons, men protect themselves ever more effectively, living in well-heated houses, riding in snug cars. The noise of their traffic penetrates whatever there may be of green spaces with growing plants and trees. Only now and then do the forever untameable elements manifest themselves in fire, floods, or tempest in the sheltering towns.

Too easily are forgotten both the work and the wisdom of men 'that go down to the sea in ships' or live, with and for all seasons, on the farms. It is of these that remote areas such as Cornwall perpetually remind us. We need, too, the wild spaces little touched by human labour. Nowhere better than in Cornwall can one feel the mysterious link between man and the whole of his planet, down to the very substance of its rocky foundations.

Here I learned to respect the power of the sea, the fury of the wind, and to adore, every year afresh, fragile, young, green life springing from brown soil. Here, though one may surmise that in aeons of time all this will come to an end, none the less, feeling myself a part of it, one with it all, I have my share in eternity. To live a life so regimented as never to know this experience is to miss something that is essential to being human.

Part Ten

THE BIOLOGICAL STRENGTH OF WOMEN

1973

Again and again Dora Russell confronts the possibility that biological differences play a role in the development of female and male consciousness. As in the past, she recognises that her stand today might not prove to be popular with many feminists who do not wish to add fuel to the flames of prejudice by 'providing' an argument that sexual inequality can be reduced to biological explanations – and is therefore inevitable. For Dora Russell, the recognition of biological difference does *not* lead to conclusions of biological determinism; it is simply a factor which must be taken into account when trying to explain how it is that women and men have different views of the world. To omit this consideration is, to her mind, to omit essential evidence and to have only a partial account of the relationship between the sexes. But if she is adamant about including biological considerations she is equally adamant about not misusing this evidence (in the way that it has so often been misused – against women – in the past). The fact that men have been unable to use women's biological uniqueness against them does not make it necessary for women to repudiate this uniqueness as far as Dora Russell is concerned; only under male dominance, she argues, could maternity be viewed as a weakness, but this is a reason for ending male dominance, not for denying the biological considerations of maternity. In her view, women should reclaim their reproductive capacity, not deny it.

THE BIOLOGICAL STRENGTH OF WOMEN

With great pleasure I read in the latest number of *Women Speaking*, October 1973, that section of Dr Eliot Slater's lecture on 'Biological Differences and Social Justice' which dealt with sex and equality. This article impressed me immensely when I read it in the *New Statesman*; I regretted that, in the subsequent correspondence, that journal concerned itself with the subject of relative black and white intelligence, and not with the interesting points of sex difference which Dr Slater raised.

It is fashionable, as he pointed out, more and more to equate men and women as 'persons' who acquire their masculine and feminine attributes by education in 'role playing', their biological differences being, as far as possible, ignored. This was very much the attitude shown in the perfunctory discussion on the status of women at the recent Liberal party conference in England this autumn of 1973. Everyone in the political world to-day is scared to admit the female function of child-bearing, with the exception of the dyed-in-the-wool reactionary, who would still like to send women back to the kitchen sink. The tendency is part and parcel of our industrial functional society, which treats men and women workers as cogs in the machine – and, ultimately, nothing but statistical units. I regard this as dangerous, as I view the whole of our modern objectives, just because it signifies a flight from the biological basis of all human life, not only that of women.

I appreciate fully the claims that women have made to enter what is called man's world, to do any work for which their skill and intelligence equip them, to avoid always being relegated to women's jobs, or to matters that are said to

167

belong to women's world. But that there is *no such thing* as two *separate* worlds for men and women, never seems to occur to anyone nor to enquire how it is that this separation of the sexes and hostility between them ever came about. This question has been worrying me for close on fifty years, but I long ago reached the conclusion that the answer must be sought in biology rather than politics.

If you ask any of our pundits what are the motives underlying political action, some will say lust for power, others economic forces, materialistic determinism by the means of production; some perhaps religious sectional interests, or more rarely, idealistic hopes of improving the human condition. No one hitherto ever looked at sex.

Yet the relation of the sexual differences between men and women to the rearing of their offspring, – the foundation of the family, – is obviously the beginning of social and economic life. Social harmony and happiness could flow from the co-operation and adjustment of these two differing sexual and parental needs. Why then do we have a world in which for centuries men have oppressed, enslaved, cruelly treated and insulted women?

When I began, in 1926, to write a book in which I wanted to sketch a social system based upon human biological needs, contrasting this with the existing system,* it seemed to me that the dualism of mind and matter, soul and body, was the chief source of what was wrong with our society, in that it led to repressing the creative force of instinct and to basing our laws and institutions on abstractions. I have not space here to go into my whole argument.

Pursuing this idea further, I saw this dualism as clearly derived from the philosophy and religion of men, since there was no sign that women had ever had any part in shaping it. It rested in fact on the sexual nature of men. The sex drive in man is, while it lasts, imperative, an urgent and immediate need of a woman. But when satisfied, in the period of quiescence, there comes the moment of sadness or revulsion in the male, when he feels released and free to exercise his other faculties. The notion of the mind or the soul emerges; he

* *The Right To Be Happy*, 1927 (see pp. 45–63 above).

does not ask himself what goes on in the woman, whom he relegates to serving his own physical need, resenting the fact that there are times when he cannot do without her. But he proceeds to do this, in so far as he can, by keeping her in ignorance and seclusion, shut out from the public world in which he alone can legislate and rule. Some people have held that the enslavement of women came about when men first discovered their own part in begetting children, whose birth was not, therefore, some miracle of female fertility. This may be so; since as men became involved in providing for children, the desire to be certain of their paternity may have arisen. But I believe that the true basis for men's hostility to and repression of women, is resentment at dependence on women as sex partners, and as the maternal source of safety and care during childhood. This would also explain the masculine insistence on taking a boy away from his mother as soon as possible, in order to make a man of him.

It is obviously not possible to guess how civilisation might have developed had women and not men been the dominant sex. Women were forced to accept the male view of sexuality, to be ashamed of their earthly desires; to become frigid; to take on many disguises foreign to their nature. In consequence we have today an intense and increasing interest among women in the nature of their own sexuality.

This long disquisition is intended to express gratitude to Dr Slater for the light that his insight brings to these problems. It meant much to me to read him, after my own fumblings. I believe the biological strength of women to be a very relevant factor in politics; we are women, not merely 'role players'.

If we look at the effect of the mind—matter dualism not only on religion and philosophy, but on the direction of scientific theory and enquiry and the practical results in applied science, it would appear possible to argue that the whole of our modern technological system rests, ultimately, upon the sexual nature of man. It came to be assumed that the whole essence of man was in his soul, or spirit, or reason. It was the duty and destiny of man to dominate, not only the animal desires of his own body, but the rest of creation, the animal and material world. In the study of science, in the observation of the material world, emotional reactions must be set aside and an impartial attitude prevail. More and more man moves into the cold atmosphere of concepts, abstractions, mathematics, planning. And, since the suppression of all kinds of emotion is a hard discipline, rage and violence erupt.

I am not denying the immense achievements of the human intellect and what it has done to advance material civilisation, nor that this achievement has been almost entirely masculine. This is precisely what is wrong with it. Nor am I suggesting that women do not have minds, in exactly the same sense as men have minds. But it has been largely through the devoted physical service of women that men have been set free to use their minds to good purpose. They have also used them to bad purpose, having refused to face the extent to which their despised and repressed passions were the very forces driving the intellect on to achieve. Anger, rivalry, fear, hatred, greed, pride took their toll. Where was love, where compassion? Sometimes, as civilisation slowly advanced, bestowed on that lowly creature woman and her brood; but there was no place for these emotions in the world of power and secular affairs.

Here is where I join issue with the advocates of 'role-playing' by men and women as 'persons' in an ordered rational society. Posturing, creating 'images' are very much the features of a society that has come adrift from its moorings. We are women, not role players, and our biological strength has never been more relevant to politics than in this present age. To abdicate before technology in excelsis rampant, is treason to civilisation.

I am not suggesting that we should play the old maternity card 'women and children first'. Nor need we enslave men to support the unlimited products of our fertility. But, in discarding the notion of sex as sin, and taking account of our own bodily impulses, we can also discard the trumpery cardboard images of ourselves set up in an affluent consumer conscious society. Then we will be able to remind men that they, like us, are animal beings living on a very lovely but limited planet. That we have a relation to everything else on the planet; that men are not the Lords of Creation, but are mismanaging their own lives and those of others very badly. That it is time they took stock of themselves and their purposes. What do they think they are doing in this world, anyway? And why have they gone on, down the ages, 'going it alone', making life ever more selfish, chilly and desolate, when help from the strength and warmth of the partner at their side was there for the asking?

Will they not swallow their pride and listen to what we are saying? Even the old Scripture said 'male *and female* created he them'.

Part Eleven

THE LONG
CAMPAIGN

1974

Dora Russell's feminism is amply illustrated in this illuminating
article, which was her opening address at the Rationalist Press
Association Conference in Oxford.

THE LONG CAMPAIGN

The changing role and attitude of women in our society has been of recent years a constant topic in the press, on television and in numerous able books. At our conference this week-end there will doubtless be no lack of theories as to the true nature of woman, what she is, was, and what she ought to be. The title of my contribution – not made by me – implies that, being somewhat advanced in years, I can give some account of woman's long struggle to reach her present status. What part will she play from now on in our social system? To ask that question is to provoke another: what is and what will be the shape of our society itself? For this, too, has now become the subject of anxious questioning and heart-searching. I propose, therefore, to start with the new society and its origins.

Individuals in our society have their being at various stages of our culture; some still live in the Middle Ages, others in the Renaissance or the eighteenth century; few are true twenty-first-century moderns. The same variety still obtains in many of our laws and customs. If, for instance you are a devout believing Christian, with an intense relation to a personal God, the shape of the universe can matter little to you; you might just as well be living in the closed medieval world with our earth as the centre. If you were, like so many educated men, reared on the classics, it is the shape of the Greek world that appeals. But for most people in advanced industrial societies the concept of the universe called up by the imagination is that of the orbiting planets keeping their time and place as calculated and expounded by the great Isaac Newton, and ordained by God.

Look upward, when thy mind on earth's confusion
　　　　　　　ponders
And mark the steadfast stars, not one from duty wanders.

Researching in eighteenth century thought I became
fascinated by the effect on men's minds of their loss of
cosiness, that alarming moment when they had to visualise
their earth, a not very important speck, whirling away
among others through the vast starry spaces, the centre of
their universe now the sun. Mankind's adjustment had to be
– and certainly was – phenomenal. Mathematics and science
had come on the scene to begin the interminable wrangle
with traditional religion.

Since the dawn of consciousness man has shaped his
mode of life and later the structure of his society and laws in
accordance with his beliefs about his environment and the
nature and actions of gods whom he feared or worshipped.
Suddenly it occurred to me – more than fifty years ago – that,
transferring his worship to a God now seen as the great
Clockmaker regulating a smoothly running universe, man
would likewise seek to emulate him. There would be what I
called a new 'religion of the machine age'. 'Give me matter
and motion,' cried Descartes, 'and I will construct the world.'
There was born the eighteenth century dream of 'natural
laws' spreading uniformity and harmony, of steady human
progress through time, of the perfectibility of man when at
last released from old phobias and superstitions. This Gospel
of the Enlightenment inspired the American Revolution,
which drew upon eighteenth century European thought. It
gave promise for man of a new beginning, in which the
bedrock of certainty was science. Such a belief was also basic
for Marxists, who claimed that their theory of the inevitable
development of human society was, by contrast with all other
political theories, scientific. What struck me when I was in
Russia in 1920 was that here was a people who had not gone
through the Reformation or the Enlightenment, but – being
in a sense at the Renaissance stage – had adopted the new
religion wholesale. Their view of the State, which, once the
mechanism had been set up and was running well, would
presently 'wither away', fitted perfectly into the pattern. In

a controversy with American Marxists in 1920 I wrote:

> Since Newton, religious thought has tended to take refuge in the notion of the First Cause; God becomes merely a clockmaker or cinematograph operator turning a handle, no longer closely concerned with individual lives or with individual desires. He is the impersonal origin of the laws by which the Universe is regulated, laws which are strictly impartial and no more favourable to man than the rest of creation. I believe this to be the instinctive religion of the average modern mind: though not formulated as a dogma, it dominates the imagination. With it goes a passionate belief in the solidity and importance of matter, likewise derived ultimately from the Newtonian gravitation theory. Good, or rather goods, come to that man who sufficiently understands the working of natural laws to achieve material prosperity by their means.
>
> The modern theory of the State derives, like the old one, from the current religious conception. It envisages the ruler, or group of rulers, as scientific winders of the clock, who construct society according to certain fixed laws regulating the distribution of matter, in complete disregard of ranks and classes, prayers of individuals, or received moral standards. This, I think is what is meant by the exclusion of the 'ethico-deific' argument [as frequently used then by Marxists].
>
> Instead, therefore, of a 'divine' right of kings, we have, as it were, a 'mechanical' right of kings, and opposition to the mechanism is an abominable heresy. Criticism of men like Lenin is as absurd as criticism of the impartial First Cause, since they are no more responsible for the social upheavals involved in their clock-winding, than God for the earthquakes occurring in his well-regulated universe. Further to object that the State was made for man and not man for the State is as antiquated a superstition as the pretension that the universe was made by God as a comfortable dwelling place for humanity. All that we can do, in both cases, is to sigh and wish that the Creator had spent his time on anything but creating.

I have never believed in Marxist communism as a science,

nor in the materialist conception of history, nor in material progress as a sole aim. What I am trying to say here is that the majority to-day still live and act according to this machine age religion; decade after decade it has fulfilled its material promise in factories, railroads, cars, motorways, all the appurtenances of our technological society, embodying a persecuting industrial faith now imposing itself in the far corners of the earth. Nowadays there are some who speak sceptically of 'living within Newtonian cosmology', implying a disbelief which I have long also held. But see the grip which this religion has upon the mind in, for instance, this passage from Professor J. H. Plumb's recent book *The Death of the Past*:

> Industrial society, unlike the commercial craft and agrarian societies which it replaces, does not need the past. Its intellectual and emotional orientation is towards change rather than conservation, towards exploitation and consumption. The new methods, new processes, new forms of living of scientific and industrial society have no sanction in the past and no roots in it. The past becomes, therefore, a matter of curiosity, of nostalgia, a sentimentality. Of course, vestiges of its strength remain, particularly in religion and politics, which are still in conflict and in crisis within the new advanced industrial societies.

Or see what it does to Ernest Gellner's concept of education in his book *Thought and Change*:

> Villages in general do not have the resources to produce anything but second class, merely potential citizens. The manufacture [his word] of a human being requires more than the resources of family and village, it requires the resources of an educational system . . . the minimal requirement for full citizenship, for effective moral membership of a modern community, is literacy . . . a certain level of technical competence is probably also required. Only a person possessing these can really claim and exercise his rights, can attain a level of affluence and style of life

compatible with current notions of human dignity.

The idea that to be illiterate is to be immoral strikes me as very odd.

Professor Christopher Hill, who is, I believe, a Marxist, in his book *God's Englishman* contrasts the stability and spiritual strength of the medieval village within the widespread acceptance of the Roman Catholic Church and its reassuring ritual of confession and absolution with the solitary Protestant conscience perforce seeking alone to read God's purposes and laws. He sees the scientific consensus as a substitute for a powerful religious orthodoxy. In the world of 'scientific certainties':

the desperate search for God has ended by squeezing Him right out of the universe. And science is a collective activity. Knowledge is pooled. Man can again share his certainties with a community and he is no longer passively at the mercy of a hostile material and social environment, he can control them both within extensible limits. The individual need no longer bear the sky on a single pair of shoulders. An approach to the world which in [the 17th century] period produced a Luther, a Descartes, a Milton, a Bunyan, to-day produces psychiatric cases.

If, however, you are neither a Roman Catholic nor a believer in the Marxist scientific consensus, you will still have to take the sky on your shoulders and hope to escape insanity.

We all know that the work of Einstein on space-time, matter and energy, changed, for those who could understand it, the picture of the universe, that the atom-splitters have abolished the old solidity of matter. But to grasp these theories and estimate their possible effects on our daily lives requires a high degree of training and intelligence. Only a minority of thinking and conscientious people even as yet comprehend the effect of the atom bomb on warfare. Einstein still had some sense of being in tune with Divine purpose, he felt that the 'Old One' must accept and fit in with his calculations. But C. P. Snow, who keeps abreast of the relation between scientific discovery and ordinary human thought and action, puts into the mouth of a young scientist in his novel *The Malcontents* these words:

> If there are any universal laws for the cosmos they must be very difficult. So difficult that it looks as if we may never know them . . . I don't think the universe is ever going to look beautiful again. No more nice beautiful simple generalisations like Einstein's . . . if you like, you can say that our minds are too simple to cope.

H. G. Wells was revered in my generation as the great prophet of the machine age. All his life he fought for a more humane, rational, civilised world within what he fundamentally did believe to be a universe which had some purpose. I have always been surprised that the final prophecies of the imagination that could produce *The Shape of Things to Come* – set out in his last book *Mind at the End of Its Tether* – were greeted with such condescending and disparaging comment. Always infuriated by human folly and muddle, seeing science turned increasingly to destruction, H. G. finally gave way to pessimism and envisaged the universe as hostile to man. He bids farewell to Newtonian cosmology:

> Hitherto events have been held together by a certain logical consistency as the heavenly bodies as we know them have been held together by the pull, the golden cord, of gravitation. Now it is as if that cord had vanished and everything was driving anyhow to anywhere at a steadily increasing velocity . . . events now follow one another in an entirely untrustworthy sequence . . . but no one but a modern scientific philosopher can accept this untrustworthiness fully.

Of man himself he says:

> Man must go steeply up or down and the odds seem to be in favour of his going down and out. If he goes up, so great is the adaptation demanded of him that he must cease to be a man. Ordinary man is at the end of his tether. Only a small highly adaptable minority of the species can possibly survive. The rest will not trouble about it, finding such opiates and consolations as they have a mind for.

For me this is exactly where we stand to-day. Another cosy – or at least comprehensible – world is gone. That small scientific élite alone know how to cope with all this 'untrustworthiness' of the universe; for us ordinary mortals nothing remains but either to trust and serve that élite, or seek 'such opiates and consolations as we have a mind for.' Which is precisely what masses of human beings are doing everywhere to-day. We may, perhaps, comfort ourselves with the thought that, as a matter of historical record, if we still care about history, it is usually the humble underlings brought in to do the dull and dirty work, who, in the end, take over from their masters.

You will by now be asking me impatiently where and when in all this does woman come in. The answer is nowhere. Though there have been educated woman, and rare periods when women have become rulers, the astounding fact of human history is that religion and philosophy, political, social and economic thought have been reserved as the prerogative of man. Our cultural world is thus the product of male consciousness. By spiritual insight he sought his god, by intellect he planned government and sought to understand his environment. Man divorced himself from the animal world, thereby creating a dualism which reinforced such aggression as he needed for survival. Even when Darwin brought him face to face with his ape ancestors it did not occur to man to study himself as an animal. Not only the religious, but even atheists, stood on their human dignity – 'to behave like an animal' has always been a term of abuse. One echo of *The Origin of Species* is aggressive nationalism derived from the struggle for survival.

The most colossal error in human history was the relegation of woman to the animal kingdom, the denial to her of a soul and mind and thus a share in the purposes of man. Robert Graves expressed a profound truth when he wrote:

In my view the political and social confusion of these last 3,000 years has been entirely due to man's revolt against woman as a priestess of natural magic, and his defeat of her wisdom by the use of intellect.

That Freud shook reliance on the intellect and indicated the impulses that underlie and more often than not actually direct it – is to-day a mere platitude. But *why* has humanity had to carry down the centuries this burden of sex as sin, and *why* for centuries have men oppressed, enslaved, cruelly treated and insulted women?

Elaine Morgan in her remarkable book *The Descent of Woman* seeks an explanation far back in some results of the change in coital posture. I think that maybe it starts quite simply from the nature of man's sexual impulse. Here, please understand I am dealing with this in vacuo, without reference to all the social, economic and romantic factors that have accrued to it. The sex drive in man is, while it lasts, an urgent and immediate need of a woman. But when satisfied, in quiescence, comes the moment of 'sadness' or revulsion in the male. He feels released and free to exercise other faculties – the notion of his mind and soul emerges. He does not ask himself what goes on in the woman, whom he sees merely as serving his own physical need and he even resents the fact that he cannot do without her. (I believe that the male attitude later extended to include resentment at childhood dependence on the mother.) Woman, he feels, is dragging him back into that animal world from which he seeks to escape, hence she is something low and vile, to be used only when sex or the need to beget offspring dictates. 'It is better to marry than to burn.' Thousands of examples of this familiar attitude could be quoted, but few realise how very deeply it is implanted in man. In Tolstoy's early diaries – he is regarded as one of the world's great men – girls are, for him (at the age of 19) 'evil influences', the company of women a necessary social evil to be avoided whenever possible.

> Who indeed [he writes] is the cause of sensuality, indolence frivolity and all sorts of other vices in us, if not women? Who causes us to lose our natural qualities of courage, reason and justice, if not women?

> 'The woman tempted me and I did eat,' said Adam.

What concerns me is a very different aspect of the flight from the body. The dualism of man's nature, expressed in religion and philosophy, proceeds to scientific study, in which emotional reactions must be set aside and an impartial attitude prevail. Man moves further and further into the cold atmosphere of concepts, abstractions, mathematics, planning. It is possible to argue that the entire modern technological system rests, ultimately on the *sexual* nature of man. In a very real sense it is a man's world. Hence the definition of a human being tacitly accepted by feminists when they fought for the vote – as a rational person who takes political decisions without regard to sex. Hence also the functional society, based no longer on family and tribal relations, but on work done for money earned by each individual, whether man or woman. We have not yet reached total disregard of sex differentiation in employment, but we are moving in that direction. Paradoxically, with all our modern sexual permissiveness, the entire basis of our advanced industrial systems is a flight from sex. And since to suppress emotion and reach out for impartiality and accuracy in thought and daily work imposes too severe a discipline, rage and violence inevitably underlie our social structure. Conflict is the very essence of what man has chosen to make of his sexual nature. And he has sought to impose an identical pattern on woman whom emphatically it does not fit.

I say, with all earnestness, that this is the heart of the problem, as between individuals and in society as a whole. Civilisation does not rest upon motorcars or nuclear power, but upon two sexes, man and woman, who have never yet learned fully to understand and love one another.

When I first came into the campaign for women's rights I was not quite old enough to take part in the battle for the vote, but this was my inspiration. We were still very correct feminine women in those days; we put up our hair to show we were grown up, wore laced and boned corsets and long inconvenient clothes – an awful hindrance in fights with the police. We had to pretend that being wives and mothers was irrelevant, otherwise the heckler would tell us to go back to the kitchen. We had to imitate man in education, modes of thought, career ambition – to prove ourselves as good as a man. As I wrote in my first book *Hypatia*, 'women won the vote as a reward for their services in helping the destruction of their offspring' i.e. in the '14–18 war. Though postwar opportunities for work increased for women, in the main they were sacked from their 'war work' jobs. A professional single woman risked losing her job if she were not chaste, she lost it for certain when she married. Girls were not supposed to know anything about sex or the insides of their bodies; most of us never heard a four letter word. Married women were, of course, employed in factories, to the detriment of themselves and their children, but even they, on the whole, were considered inconvenient by employers. It was not decent to talk about sex; the marriage laws were such that no intelligent self-respecting young woman of my generation felt able to marry without feeling degraded.

Recently I read, with some emotion, what Isadora Duncan said on this subject in her *Life*. At the time when I was involved in my own divorce – around 1933 – a Bill before our Parliament proposing release from marriage when a partner had been insane for five years, failed to pass and was held to destroy 'the sanctity of the marriage bond.'

The battle of those ten years from 1920 to 1930 should not, I think, be forgotten now in the advance of Women's Liberation. So many issues claimed the energies of intelligent women. There was – and still is – that difference of opinion as to whether women should embark on public life as 'persons' or as 'women.' That a Councillor or an MP must embrace all human affairs was not denied, but there seemed no point in pressing for women candidates if they were not to bring a fresh point of view to the political arena. At one of the celebrations of winning the vote I heard a woman MP say that for her, this was just a career, whilst Mrs Pethick Lawrence spoke of women's emancipation as a pledge and part of the liberation of all underdogs.

In 1923 the police in England seized, as obscene, Margaret Sanger's pamphlet advising working class women on methods of birth control, which was being sold by Rose Witcop and Guy Aldred. Margaret Sanger herself, had much earlier fled from the United States to escape imprisonment under the Comstock Laws. She went to prison many times later in the same cause. I became angry that women who needed to limit their families were not allowed necessary advice and information. I contacted Maynard Keynes and we took the case to appeal at Quarter Sessions, mainly to ventilate the issue, for there was little chance of success. We briefed Counsel and had St Loe Strachey prepared to be a witness, whom, however, the Bench refused to hear. The pamphlet said, among other things, that women should have pleasure in sexual intercourse, a point which, I observed, was displeasing to the Bench, who were, perhaps, thinking of their wives and daughters. There was also a diagram showing how, with the finger, to place a Dutch pessary in the vagina. Obscenity, we were advised, lay in the fact that this might not be the woman's own finger. Not having a sufficiently dirty mind, this had not occurred to me or to others. We lost, of course, but the pamphlet was re-issued in 1924 under the then Labour Government, but without the offending diagram. This case convinced me that we had to enter the political arena *as women*, and that, so far from evading the issue of sex and maternity, there could be no true freedom for women without the emancipation of mothers. Marie Stopes had courageously started a birth control clinic; she had also begun to break the sex taboo by her book *Married Love*. I found a number of young women in the Labour Movement who felt as I did about the Sanger pamphlet: we embarked on a political birth control campaign about which very little is known to-day. We held – at that date a strange opinion – that a woman has the right to decide how many children she would have and therefore should receive – as of right – contraceptive advice as an integral part of the service of Maternity and Child Health. We enlisted the support of well-known people like H. G. Wells and Julian Huxley, and of Labour MPs and councillors, who moved resolutions in Parliament and local councils. We took a deputation to the Labour Minister of Health in 1924, who, as a Catholic, was not helpful. At the Labour Women's Conference of 1924, in the teeth of platform opposition, we passed by a thousand votes to eight the famous resolution containing our birth control demand, and earned a headline in the *Daily Express* '*MOTHERHOOD MENACE*.' We scrutinised maternal death rates, estimated figures for illegal abortions. Our slogan was 'It is four times as dangerous to bear a child as to work in a coal mine.' In fact, in congested industrial areas, the rate was eight or nine times as great. By the Spring of

1926, some twenty-three local councils and Maternity Committees were supporting our demand and pressuring the Ministry of Health; that year we referred back the recommendation of the Executive of the Labour Conference on the issue with block Trade Union support. May I remind you that *not until* 1967 did a Bill embodying our original demands, promoted by Edwin Brooks MP, finally pass the House of Commons, and then it was only permissive as far as local authorities were concerned. We have had the reform of the law about abortion, which we, in our time, would have supported, but it was an even more difficult cause then than contraception. The continuing intensity of present opposition to that law, will indicate something of what we faced in the 1920s. I was literally flabbergasted at the callousness of doctors, religious leaders and politicians; I wrote my book *Hypatia* in defiance, asserting woman's right to knowledge, as to sex life. The *Sunday Express* reviewer said the book ought to be banned: it sold 600 copies in a week.

I saw child-bearing and rearing as the bedrock of civilisation, yet mothers, despite sentiment about maternal joys, were the most despised and neglected section of society. Indeed it came as a great shock to many when that Labour Women's Conference revealed such powerful opposition to having babies. I find it very comical nowadays to read that the best way to check the population explosion in the less affluent countries is to raise the general standard of living – the quickest route to smaller or non existent families is to liberate the women and give them the chance to think for themselves.

I was not the only champion of mothers in the 1920s of course – there was Eleanor Rathbone, Margaret Macmillan, Sylvia Pankhurst.

The next logical step was to look at the nurture and education of children, to attempt to liberate them from the doctrine of having been born in sin. This led to Bertrand Russell and myself starting our much maligned school. Seeing children as an oppressed class, I wrote my book *In Defence of Children* in 1932.

Many of my colleagues in the birth control fight turned to founding more voluntary clinics. I was disappointed, for I believed that this was a political battle that could have been won with a hard drive.

I became involved with Dr Norman Haire, who deserves to be remembered, in the Sex Reform movement as a whole. We had the World League for Sex Reform, for which Norman and I, with Professor Jack Flügel, organised a Congress in London in 1929. At this now forgotten Congress there were 350 delegates from at least 25 countries; every country in Europe, except Portugal, but *not* excepting the Soviet Union, was represented. Two Russians read papers, the German contributions were many and learned. Contact with the Russians was important; in 1929 they were ahead of the West on marriage laws and abortion; they brought with them a film used widely to educate their women on childbirth and the danger of abortion unless done by a qualified surgeon, which was then already legal in their country. Norman and I had great fun evading the Press for a private show of this film, which could not then have passed the Censor. Dr Magnus Hirschfeld, President of the League and Head of his remarkable Institute for Sexual Research in Berlin, opened the Congress, followed by Cyril Joad, and numerous contributions including one by Bertrand Russell and ending with Bernard Shaw. The list of participants includes virtually every man or woman in Britain of what might be called the intellectual avant-garde: I daresay that many of them alive to-day might be surprised to be reminded that they were there.

That Congress passed many resolutions some of which have, even now, not been implemented. Our gospel at that time, which was then spreading fairly rapidly, was that Sex Reform and understanding could be the foundation of a humane, tolerant and peaceful world. The Congress was the peak of the progressive movement in Europe that had begun in 1918. Reaction began to move in. By 1933 Hitler was in power in Germany; Hirschfeld's Institute went up in smoke. What happened to the status of women in Germany is notorious. But in the next troubled period women's liberation in general received a set back, from which it is only now beginning to recover.

More important than the piecemeal struggle for rights is

surely the ideal of seeing men and women side by side on equal terms, taking top level decisions together. To acquire equal status as part of a revolutionary movement can give women a better start, though it takes time for custom to catch up with the political decision. Much interesting information about women's status in communist countries is available, which is not, unfortunately, due to political prejudice, better known. The incursion of women into industry, public health, education, business and local government in such countries as Albania, North Korea, North Vietnam is literally amazing: often their share is more than 50 per cent. At the North Vietnamese Women's Congress in March 1974, Le Duan, First Secretary of the Workers' Party, speaking of the New Woman in Socialist Society, accepted the principle of equal partnership when he said:

> To emancipate women is in essence to ensure their fullest participation as collective masters in all three respects: to be masters of society, masters of nature, and masters of themselves.

We could do with some encouraging words like those from some of our male politicians at home.

In our society there is much talk of 'role learning' and much confusion about the images imposed on women, who, in the end, do not really know who they are and what they want. After so many years, I have seen – what I long hoped for – young women – in the literature of Women's Lib – trying to understand themselves and make others understand them. One aspect of this is their probe into their own sexual nature. We hear quite a lot about orgasms. Since I believe that sex is basic to any deliberation about our social structure, I think that they are right. I only want to deal with one obvious fact, which, oddly enough, is still too often ignored, that for a women the sex act and child-bearing are two totally different, though both biological functions.

On the biological plane there is no conflict here; conflict between sex and maternity is introduced by contraception. The primal nature of woman is harmonious, proceeding from coitus to pregnancy, from birth to feeding the young and hunting for their food. That woman is closer to the animal world than man is her virtue, not her sin. The impulse of parental care starts from the mother and the ultimate source of creative love is her defence of the life of her offspring. Thus, while a woman may think and reason as well as any man and deal with abstractions, the end purpose of her thought will not be the same as his. Though our species must prey on other species to live, to prey upon itself for greed, power or glory, is a misdirection. That one primal instinct – residing in woman – which can go beyond self-preservation to care for others and can issue as compassion or as altruistic concern for the future, has been excluded or allocated a secondary role throughout history.

By this I do not suggest that women should all embrace maternity or involve themselves only in what relates to it, especially not in the face of the population explosion. In our complex society there should be a variety of activities that are worth pursuing. But I do sense a certain danger that now we begin to see children as 'superfluous products' we may lose immediate love for children and concern for posterity. Those qualities which women, at their best, have displayed within the family, are needed in the body politic.

We are all living in the present, with implied contempt for the past, disregard and some fear of the future. Where then do we go from here? According to some recent radio broadcasts of the BBC only into the next world and life beyond death. Biologists tell us that we are here by pure chance. So what? Others say that now there is no God there is no purpose in life. So what? Surely our purposes are our own?

Loss of faith in the machine age religion carries with it loss of faith in the functional political-economic systems to which it gives rise; it leads to disillusion with its multitude of goods and gadgets, as with its crazy money gambling games – mortgages, profits, dividends, inflation. No wonder that many young people are looking for new or old cults and religions, or indeed that large numbers of them begin to see virtue in being poor. The youthful violence that erupts is the response to be expected in a system regimented and planned by arid thought in disregard of the pent up strength of human emotions. We should be thankful rather than the reverse, for those young people who express this hunger for fellowship and animal warmth by peaceable congregation at pop festivals. They are teaching a simple lesson about brotherhood and sisterhood which we and all our churches, scientists and statesmen have forgotten.

If women are to rule side by side with men in the State, it must not be that State which men alone have fashioned and which to-day fills so many of us with dismay. Whatever may be their ambition to prove themselves the equals of men, women should be thinking hard as to what contribution they can make to the purposes and beliefs on which our new civilisation will be founded. By setting himself free for thought man, by himself, has achieved marvels, but at great cost; in the loss of the creative strength of love and compassion, the fostering, through repression, the eruption of forces of destruction. Our generation has been able to look upon the desolate moon, from there to take stock of our small finite planet. We begin to realise some of our limitations; our close relation to, our responsibility for the animal life and resources on and within our earth. As we turn back, as I hope, to biological values, there is a great opportunity for the co-operation of the sexes, to abandon the conflict implicit in the dualism of mind and body, to live as whole human beings, in understanding and full enjoyment of one another and in mutual love and concern for our children. Two aims might flow from the creative fusion of male and female thought, the destruction of the fetiches of money and of power. We could gradually create a great volume of opinion and belief which, like the medieval church though not belligerent, would be strong enough to protect individuals and give pause to the holders of power; we could gradually diminish love of and traffic in money and presently bring about the complete abolition of usury. I cannot here elaborate on these themes, but I am convinced that some great revolutionary humanist beliefs must come about if we are to survive. To achieve this I hope that the long campaign of woman through history to reach her rightful place will contribute fully; that man will no longer alone 'take the sky on his shoulders', but turn to the earth, his mother; that woman will cease to be drudge or parasite and share with dignity the shaping of a people and destiny worthy the name of human.

Part Twelve

THREATS TO FREEDOM

1978

The following article needs no introduction. It was originally delivered as a paper at the Rationalist Press Association conference on 11 September 1978.

THREATS TO FREEDOM

When we think about freedom most of us are quite sure that at the present time we do not have enough of this desirable commodity; hence we tend to look to a future when it will abundantly flourish, or, nostalgically, to a past when, we feel convinced, we were all more free than we are now. I want first of all to speak of the past, partly because of my age, but also because past experience can throw some light upon what battles may still be to come. There will soon be nobody left who can remember, at first hand, the Europe that existed before 1914. I say Europe advisedly, for I think that most Europeans believed at that time that, to all intents and purposes, *they were* the world. Perhaps they still do think so. Leonard Woolf in his autobiography has written how, after that date with destiny 1914, it has been 'down hill all the way'. Certainly before that war broke out, the upper and middle classes in England enjoyed perhaps a greater liberty than either before or since. For the working classes things were, and had been, somewhat different.

But the words 'liberty', 'equality', 'fraternity' have been echoing down among the peoples of Europe since the 18th century; and it was to defend democracy that we said we went to war in 1914. To set men free was the theme song of poets and writers, even of some statesmen, and certainly of the would-be statesmen. 'Man is born free,' cried Rousseau, 'and everywhere he is in chains.' 'You have nothing to lose but your chains' cried the revolutionary leaders of the proletariat. 'We must be free or die, who speak the tongue that Shakespeare spoke' wrote one poet, while another exhorted England to arise, dispel the web of lies woven over her face, and break the unjust laws that bound her to the ground. From the pen of Bertrand Russell, even during the '14/18 war, came a small book called *Roads to Freedom*.

There seems little doubt that men and women in this country have cherished freedom as an ideal above almost all others; a truth which applies to a very great many, though I would hesitate to say *all* peoples of the world.

Very recently the BBC put out a television programme purporting to give an account of the 1920's in this country. That happens to be my period – I came of age during the '14/18 war. I am a child of that time. What happened then and what my generation thought and did has all too often been grossly misrepresented. This BBC programme was no exception. It gave the usual nonsense about the frivolity and cynicism of the age – Noel Coward and 'Dance, dance, dance, little lady' and all that – this time attributing our so-called frivolity to a sense of shock and guilt at the appalling slaughter of the young from which Europe, with painful difficulty, was emerging. I sometimes think that misrepresentation of the twenties is deliberate, to head people off from looking at the truth.

In plain fact, the period of 1918–1929 saw an immense move forward in nearly all of the causes in which lovers of liberty believe. To begin with (though it may be said that the older politicians ought to have averted the need for that war for democracy), it is none the less true that some of the finest men of my generation died to win it. Others raised the pacifist standard, went to gaol and even died for the liberty not to kill other men in war. Next came, in 1917 the rising of the Russian people; in 1918 a near-revolution in Germany, thwarted in part by the Allied victors, unrest in Britain that alarmed those in power and did thwart the encirclement of Russia by her enemies. Those Bloomsburies, about whose sex lives present writers are having such fun, were almost all socialist or anarchist; they supported the 1917 Club and the working class. By 1924 we had a Labour Prime Minister – Ramsay MacDonald, who had been ostracised as a pacifist during the war. By 1926 we had the General Strike. The battles of women for freedom are well known. By 1924 the vote was partially won. Much more was being done on sex questions. A. P. Herbert, with wit and ridicule in his novels, and as an MP in Parliament, fought consistently to set men and women free from antiquated divorce laws. There was the fight for birth control, waged by Marie Stopes and young Labour women; for better care for mothers, for family allowances by Eleanor Rathbone. In 1923, we were defending a pamphlet by Margaret Sanger, which dared to say that women should enjoy sex, and in 1925, my own book *Hypatia* was widely sold for saying much the same thing. Concern with sex problems was becoming world wide and in 1929 we had in London a Conference of the World League for Sex Reform, supported by every country in Europe, including Russia (but excluding Portugal), and also from North and South America, Canada, India, Japan. The list of supporters in England includes virtually all of the avant garde of the day. Last but far from least, was the movement for greater freedom and experiment in education: with A. S. Neill, progressive schools, later Dartington, and there was also Geoffrey Pyke and Susan Isaacs's group of children in Cambridge.

I remind you of all this, not merely because I am tired of hearing my hard-working and public-spirited generation insulted as frivolous (just because some of us liked dancing the Charleston), but because I want to pose the question – after all this effort, what went wrong?

Did this great upsurge for freedom in politics, economics, sex and culture, simply lose momentum? Did it just decline, become obscured, or was it repressed? In our concern for freedom, we have to ask ourselves what is the most favourable climate for its advancement, or the reverse.

Another date, pointed to as significant by historians, is 1929, when there was the slump and recession in the United States, resulting, as economists have told us, in exacerbating unemployment in Britain and Germany, the Hunger Marches, Mosley's Blackshirts and the rise of Hitler. And in Spain a nascent Republic, which had only just got rid of a monarch, faced a war with reaction for whom Franco was a useful tool. Compared with the present day, the mass of the people of Europe in the 1930's were desperately poor. Can then a society not indulge in freedom and tolerance, unless it achieves a certain degree of uniform prosperity? Is it, in harsh economic circumstances, the fear of a population in revolt that prompts the reactionaries to restore 'law and order'. Or is just the very sight of people enjoying doing what they like unendurable to men and women whose own enjoyment rests in the exercise of power?

To-day, after another terrible interlude of war, we do seem to enjoy a period embodying many of the freedoms fought for in the past. People take a mere passing interest in a historical account of such past battles, because, after all, as they say, birth control, reform of abortion laws, equal pay, liberal divorce, considerable sexual freedom, a rising standard of living, are now taken for granted. At moments this attitude provokes some resentment in those who are old enough to know the bitterness of past struggles. Not that one should look for gratitude from younger generations. Rather does one feel – out of past experience – the need to issue a warning. Looking back then once more to the events from 1929 onwards, what did go wrong? Can we not now see in the signs of the times the same forces rising which, for us then, put back the clock, and extinguished the lamps of enlightenment which we, with faith in political, economic, sexual liberty, believed were lighting the path to the future?

Unlike the 1930's this is not a time of great poverty. We live in the affluent society and have been told that we never had it so good. You are free now to buy radios, washing machines, fridges, prepared frozen foods; you can lay a soft fitted carpet wall to wall, centrally heat your house. About half the population can afford to have their own car. Most people are able to afford good holidays. Is there not a great deal of liberty of all kinds? Why are we talking about threats to freedom? Why are we not content? What freedom is it that we do not possess?

One might say that we are well enough off to be tolerant. Yet in the past few years, men and women in and out of Parliament have been ganging up to alter the laws recently passed, making it possible for women to have safe and legal abortions, if they need and desire to do so. Why should these busybodies interfere in the right of choice about parenthood in the lives of others? What has it to do with them? When we fought this same kind of opposition to birth control in the 20's

I never could follow their logic or endure their brutal intolerance. And why should this generation of young women have to fight all over again for a liberty which we thought had been won for them? It is odd that those who hold it desperately wicked to destroy a foetus, are usually to be found among those who would not hesitate to destroy a whole people in nuclear war. They are all still there, these prowling hosts of Midian; they want to make us afraid of other nations, to buy more and more weapons of destruction, to breed more and more young men – and now women too – for slaughter.

Or consider the issue of education. Here many competing freedoms cause great confusion. An attempt at some kind of equality is being tried in our State schools by going comprehensive. At once those who profit by or support established privilege are on guard and very active. To whose liberty should we give priority – to the State, or society, which has certain requirements as to the citizens it wants trained; to the central Government for this reason, or to the local authorities; or to the choices and wishes of parents; or the liberty of the child to learn or not to learn, or at the very least to have some personal choice of subjects and methods of teaching?

In this maze of conflicting interests almost the only principle a rational person can advance is the freedom to experiment and try new methods. But is even this possible in the social and economic system of the present day?

In my view this is the heart of the matter. The cry that liberty is threatened is heard in these times, both from the Left and the Right. From the Right because men and women claim that something called socialism is steadily eroding their right to trade and make profits, and to spend money earned by their special ability in any way they please; not to have it filched away by the tax man. The unease of the Left is more complex. They feel that a powerful central Government takes – in secret, or without due consultation – wide reaching decisions which affect whole communities. Against the power of the big nationalised concerns the individual has next to no power of influence or redress. And the large-scale international industrial corporations are more powerful than national governments. Human beings have in fact built up a powerful bureaucratic machine based on industrial technology, in which liberty for the individual is an illusion or hypnotic trance. Individuals of both the Right and the Left fear this machine. But its hierarchical structure gives the advantage rather to the established order than to the innovator. By its very nature the machine is the enemy of democracy, a perfect instrument to hand for the war lord or dictator.

There is something very pitiful and at the same time paradoxical about the way in which, by the very pursuit of freedom, men have organised themselves into slavery. To escape from the curse of Adam – heavy and exhausting labour – was the ideal. Specialisation and the machine were to be the road to freedom. How hard was the fight, first for the ten hour, then for the eight hour day. The great Lord Shaftesbury even wished all factories and work places to close each day at 6 p.m. Where to-day are those limits of hours fought for, in the face of what may be made by double pay for many hours of overtime. In fact the more mechanised our world has become the more have liberty and leisure steadily diminished. And whereas in the past release from excessive toil was eagerly sought, now goes up the cry of the 'right to work', jobs must be created, it is a sin to leave men and women unemployed. And to prepare boys and girls for entry into the workaday world we have erected a whole system of training and examination tests of increasing severity, in which young people do seem to suffer a great deal of anxiety and strain. Setting aside what we surmise about the very extensive records about our learning capacity, character, health, political views Intelligence Agents may be feeding into the computers, have we, even ignoring all these, in our advanced industrial civilisations, any real liberty worth having?

Our social system, though created by human beings, is no longer to be assessed or measured in human terms. It seems to cater more for human vices, than human virtues – that is, for greed, rivalry and hardness of heart. Nor should we ascribe this state of affairs to the capitalist profit motive. In early stages this played some part, but the true source of our ills is the cult of the impartial scientific intellect, to the exclusion and disparagement of emotions.

We must, whether by decentralisation, or great changes in our legal and educational system, get back to a way of life in which men and women – and consequently their children – can feel free to operate in human terms. It might do us good to take a look at some of the wise advice to be found in the works of Kropotkin. We have externalised everything, we live all the time other-directed, waiting to be told what to do and what to believe. We have indeed become part of our own machine. A human being should be autonomous, composed of many complex desires and feelings – we do not live either by the direction of pure reason, or by spirit inspired by God. As well as fear and rivalry, we also have impulses to create, to form associations with others, we feel compassion and generosity. Traditionally we have been taught to be afraid of our basic animal impulses, with the result that too often it is the good, rather than the bad and destructive, which get repressed.

A society, to be called human, should, surely, take its origin from some natural impulse in men and women to come together for mutual help in the business of living. This was, I think, what Rousseau meant by his social contract and the expression of the 'general will'. I entirely disagree with those – and Bertrand Russell (in *Western Philosophy*) was one – who see in Rousseau's ideas the ultimate source of totalitarianism and even the Nazi regime. Rousseau, in fact, believed that small democracies were preferable to large states, and for him co-operation was a generous impulse of the heart. The Nazi regime had nothing to do with grass roots inspiration; it was from the top downwards, a brilliant planners' technological machine for the waging of total war. Skilful propaganda was used to whip up hatred for the Jews – and others – and to suggest and glorify a disciplined race of supermen. All this derives ultimately from the impartial abstractions which science had been preaching since the 18th century, setting the human intellect free from subjectivity, only in the end to serve destructive power. Total mechanised war is Hitler's legacy to mankind.

In his lectures on science and the Modern World, Whitehead suggests that it is the function of philosophy to be a critic of abstractions. While he accepts that it is useful, in seeking to understand nature, to deal in abstractions such as the Cartesian mind and matter, this scheme unfortunately tends to develop a mode of thought incapable of dealing with the remainder of things in experience which have been left out. 'A civilisation,' he says, 'which cannot burst through its current abstractions is doomed to sterility after a very limited period of progress.'

Thus, while I entirely accept that there are a great many measures we can take to deal with the lack or loss of liberty which we experience here and now, I do believe that prospects of liberty in the future depend on our determination and ability to rethink our approach to the human being in society and our entire relation to the natural world.

I should like in conclusion to quote from a letter written by George Sand to Flaubert in the Spring of 1872 – France, after the defeat of 1870, was in a parlous state. I feel that George Sand, the first of modern liberated women, expresses what a liberated woman may feel in these times about our own – and other countries.

Her son, knowing that his mother, then 68, would certainly ride to Paris, probably to die in the mêlée, locked the stables and forbade the servants to give her a horse.

This is no time to be sick, old troubadour, and certainly no time to grumble. What we must do is cough, wipe our noses, get well and declare – aloud, very firmly – that France is mad, humanity stupid, and we ourselves are no more than a breed of badly designed animals.

What I have just said is true as far as it goes, but there is more. We must go on being in love with ourselves, the species to which we belong, and, most of all, our friends. We cannot permit ourselves to be deflected by the insanity that surrounds us on every side, and that, if we are not careful, insidiously influences our thinking until we, too, see the world upside down.

Perhaps this chronic state of indignation is one of the necessary conditions of your continued existence, but I know it would be the death of *me*! Is it possible, you ask, to live in peace when the human race is so absurd? Speaking only for myself, which is all that my conscience permits, I am prepared to submit to the conditions of absurdity, reflecting the while that I, perhaps, am no less absurd than anyone else. What matters is that I begin to think how to improve myself, since I am unable to aid in the improvement of others.

Why then, you will ask, do we write, if it is impossible to influence the thinking of others? My dear friend, I can only reply that we are unable to influence man's destiny overnight. If our advice is sound, if the mirror we hold up to society is accurate enough for man to recognize his reflection, and little by little persuade him to change his image, then we will not have lived in vain. Nor will we have written in vain; our self-love will have served the compassionate purpose that, we like to tell ourselves, is our motive for spending our entire lives in the lonely, grinding work of creating a world on paper. (Quoted in Noel B. Gerson's biography of George Sand (Robert Hale, 1973), pp. 256–7)

Part Thirteen

FELLOW FEMINISTS

Throughout her life, Dora Russell has been inspired by other women and has supported other women. She has much praise for her contemporary, Naomi Mitchison, and declares that Alexandra Kollontai was the model for the youthful Dora. Always, Dora Russell has tried to make women's contributions visible and has taken every opportunity to review the work and the writing of women.

Naomi Mitchison, the author of many books ('over seventy-five' by her own admission) has been disgracefully neglected, but some of her work is now being reprinted (Virago) and Jill Nyce is currently writing a biography of Mitchison, which will be published by Pandora Press.

BOOK REVIEWS

All Change Here: Girlhood and Marriage
by Naomi Mitchison

Naomi Mitchison now brings the story of her life up to the end of the 1914–18 war. She and I are contemporaries. Both of us grew up in good King Edward's golden days, when food was real food, eaten and priced according to freshness and the season; fridges as yet not invented to create beef and butter mountains. There were the horse buses and the hansom cabs in which only 'fast' ladies would ride with a gentleman.

We both enjoyed a youthful boyish freedom, followed by the frustration of long skirts and young ladydom – and later went through the prolonged struggle to regain our liberty through women's emancipation. Conservative upper class conventions and beliefs enclosed Naomi's adolescence, her education was consigned to a governess, while for her brother there were Eton and Oxford. But through the work of her father J. S. Haldane, and the undergraduate milieu of her brother Jack – J. B. S. – Naomi lived at the very heart of Oxford University and early absorbed the atmosphere of scientific research. Genetic studies began with Jack and Naomi's joint keeping of guinea pigs. And at Liberal Ministerial level there was Uncle Richard – Lord Haldane. It was a rich and fascinating social life, with the young Huxleys, the Gielguds, Dick Mitchison, among many of the most brilliant young men of the time. Naomi recalls, as I do, that 'the poor were a vague concept outside our experience, relegated to the domain of "good works".' For her, through her father's scientific work for miners, came the first contact with real working men. She began to wonder and hold views which she felt it unwise to express.

The outbreak of war she describes as at first a thrilling event – a glorious adventure, which everyone believed would rapidly end in victory. One by one the young men went away to be slaughtered, devoutly believing all the patriotic propaganda on which they were fed.

At first with equal acceptance Naomi became a VAD but was too young to be sent to France. At seventeen, scarcely knowing the meaning of what she was doing, she became engaged to Dick Mitchison, a match that seems to have been approved and fostered by parents on both sides. The marriage was lasting; she mentions casually that they always wrote to each other every day! But, at eighteen, Naomi faced the full horror of a young wife in time of war. Dick was wounded in the head, with brain damage which for months was thought to be permanent. At his bedside in the French hospital she was met by him not merely with a failure of recognition, but with insults and rejection. Back in England he made what seemed a miraculous recovery. One can only admire her fortitude as indeed that of all that young generation whose lives took the full blast of the war.

Some of us came off much more lightly. I was at Girton, with little or no contact with Cambridge young men, nor had I met any in my life in suburbia. The mood of Cambridge was more sceptical than that at Oxford. There was Bertrand Russell and many other dons who were sympathetic to this stand against the war, though they did not speak out as he did. There was C. K. Ogden with the Heretics and the *Cambridge Magazine*. Patriotic fervour ran high, but dissent spoke with no uncertain voice. As Naomi began writing letters to the *Oxford Times* and helped to found the Oxford branch of the League of Nations Society, so many of us adored and followed Russell and espoused the cause of the conscientious objectors. From then on for Naomi and her husband as for me and others, came the move forward into the Labour Party and the years of political struggle for peace, equality, socialism – a better world for women as for men, which in retrospect seems to have been so rewarding and yet in the end to have achieved so little.

You May Well Ask by Naomi Mitchison

Naomi Mitchison's previous volume of autobiography *All Change Here* covered the period of the First World War. When I reviewed that book in the *New Humanist* (August 1975) I drew attention to the similarity between us, as young women growing up in a university atmosphere, she in Oxford, myself in Cambridge. Both of us watched the flower of our young men drafted off to slaughter, leaving the older generation still in power after the war.

Yet our actual personal and environmental wartime experiences differed greatly. At the age of nineteen she endured the agony of a newly married wife at the bedside of a husband so badly wounded that if he survived, it might be with severe brain damage. (Fortunately, Dick Mitchison's full recovery led to a highly successful career.) For me a brief spell of war service interrupting my studies – a Government Mission to New York with my father, Sir Frederick Black – had turned me into a convinced pacifist; while she began writing to the papers about the need to set up a League of Nations. The brilliant young men, including her brother J. B. S. Haldane, among whom she moved at Oxford were, in the main, patriotic, and her home background at least where women were concerned, was conservative. In Cambridge we rejoiced in near worship of Bertrand Russell, as a member of the older generation who stood up for the young; we also had C. K. Ogden, with the Heretics.

Perhaps I may mention another young woman contemporary of significant wartime experience and influence, Lella Sargant Florence. In 1921, with her husband Phillip, she settled in Cambridge, where they both became the centre of progressive causes, pacifism, heresy, rights of women. Lella, whose wartime letters have recently been published, came over in the Ford Peace Ship in 1916, and in 1917 (when I was 'in the war' in New York) she was there also but on the verge of a nervous breakdown at the failure of her almost incredible campaign to try and prevent America from coming in.

The lives of all three of us – young, with literary ambitions, but at first no politics – is of some interest in the years between the wars, mainly because it was a time of great change in the status of women. Significantly, as mothers, we unhesitatingly espoused the cause of birth control, Naomi helping the North Kensington clinic and Lella founding one at Cambridge.

In her new book, Naomi Mitchison, at twenty-one, wife of a professional man ambitious for a career, and mother of a young baby, faces the inescapable problems of housewife and social hostess, combined with a compulsive urge to write poetry and books. She reminds us of the economic and cultural standards taken for granted by the well-to-do of the 1920s with a domestic staff of housemaid, parlour maid, cook and nurses, making possible a full and varied social life.

The details of ordinary life rather than great events are what matter most to ordinary people; perhaps women notice these more because they are more affected by them. However that may be, I find it useful to find set down what – not so very long ago – childbirth was like; what were accepted ways of nursing infectious illness and of rearing babies; the gradual sophistication in choice and cooking of food. Class distinctions were clear; in nothing more so than in nutrition and health. 'On the whole', she says 'good health was privilege: it belonged to the middle and upper classes.' But even the privileged suffered from the absence of the medical and surgical skills of today; Naomi's eldest son aged nine, died of meningitis, from which modern anti-biotics could have saved him.

So there we were and rooms were clean and tidy, the meals were cooked and served, orders to shops delivered on time and there were at least three posts a day, all based on our being at the top end of the class structure. We could presumably have sat back and enjoyed it, but we filled up all that lovely spare time which nobody seems to have to-day, with our friends and children, our and our friends' love affairs, our good causes and committees, Dick's Bar work, my writing, interest in the other arts, letters, trips abroad and as time went on, the growth of a social conscience . . . We found ourselves living in a frame of mind where the class structure began to look very unreal.

The Mitchisons' social life was indeed extensive and remarkable. They must have given pleasure to literally thousands of all kinds of people. Bertie and I were among the guests at the Boat Race parties on the roof of River Court, with our dark or light blue badges. Innumerable large parties and the rearing of five children would have been more than enough for most women, but Naomi has immense vitality and, it would seem, good health, as well as wide-ranging curiosity.

With all that, she is by temperament an introvert; not at all a 'political animal', though she could act decisively and with courage when necessary. It was in politics that I sometimes met her; she did not join the Labour Party until 1931, disliked public speaking until, in 1934, rage at the Dollfüss government's attack on socialist Vienna spurred her to eloquence. Her beloved brother Jack Haldane's attachment to the Communist Party caused a bitter break between them – the Cold War within her own family. She did not hate the Russians, she saw them as individuals.

Relations between people, not the 'party line', the meeting of minds, the flights of the imagination are what Naomi Mitchison lives by. I doubt whether a full story of her life can be written unless it is based on what must be a treasure house of personal letters, of which she affords a glimpse in this book. Intrigued by the selection, I concluded that she wants to evoke the moods, the false dawns, of the search in those inter-war years, for a way of life, beliefs and values. E. M. Forster comments on loyalty as seen by barbarians and civilised men. It 'matters very much' to a barbarian 'to have given our heart to a person or a hope', 'where to the civilised man life is full of justifiable treacheries'; he has learnt that 'there is no consistency even in the heart.'

The barbarians of ancient Gaul, or the ancient Greeks and Romans, rather than contemporary politics, peopled Naomi Mitchison's imagination; only later did she deal with contemporary themes. Then, as is revealed by her correspondence about her book *We Have Been Warned* with even progressive publishers such as Victor Gollancz and Jonathan Cape, it was all right to deal with 'overt sex' among people wearing wolf-skins and togas, but not when you mention the smell of a shirt or rubber preventives, or undoing trouser buttons. What 'right-minded' people thought about all this appears in a letter which she received about 1939:

> Having just read *We Have Been Warned* I write to inform you that of all the thousands of books I have read it is far the filthiest. In spite of the foreword, one can only suppose it represents the views and modes of life of socialists and communist 'comrades'. Apparently murder, perjury, drunkenness, foul language and moral depravity of every sort are their stock in trade. I wonder that Constable published it. I suppose it was a bit too thick for 'Comrade Gollancz'.

Like most young women, Naomi's introduction to studying sex had been Marie Stopes's *Married Love*. Yet in the reactionary atmosphere that still prevailed, she was probably more forthright and understanding about sexual, racial and even ideological tolerance than most of her left-wing colleagues. Many of the writers and poets among her friends were homosexuals; E. M. Forster, Gerald Leach, Wystan Auden, whom she 'discovered' and helped as she did others of both sexes who lacked recognition. Sexual tolerance extended even within her own marriage, sustained over about fifty years till Dick's death, and during which both had other love affairs but wrote to each other virtually every day. Haunted by their repressive upbringing, they none the less felt the need of the freshness and stimulus of new companions in love. To this end jealousy must be ruled out as unworthy.

I sometimes hoped I was fighting for more freedom for a

whole generation of women. My daughters perhaps? Who, I dreamed, would be able to have children by several chosen fathers, uncensured. This was the kind of dream many of us had.

The book ends in 1940, when Naomi, herself pregnant, is helping the evacuation of mothers and children from Glasgow to her house Carradale and surrounding cottages in Argyll, wondering what will happen in the next fortnight and how to behave if Hitler should invade. In July, despite the attentions of a specialist, her baby died.

Discussion of this book with its author on televison and in the *Observer* showed how little is now understood about the courage of some women of her generation and the meaning of their quest in a society in which the old writs of law and morals still ran, not only in sex, but in economics. Asked on television why people so well placed as the Mitchisons became active socialists, Naomi said that they believed in fairness for all; on which I understood the interviewer to remark that this was now an antiquated liberal ideal. In both interviews the importance of the battle for sexual liberation as social policy, but still more in its personal code, was underrated.

After the First World War some women, and some of the men who managed to survive, sought a new morality to replace the old in which their elders still sat entrenched. Women began to hope that values which they felt to be theirs by right now prevail: cooperation instead of rivalry and war; compassion to be applied to relieve poverty and improve the people's health, to succour overburdened mothers. There should be new ideals of child nurture and education; sex should no longer be dirty and secret, the expression of love should not be subject to property and possession. An attempt could be made to overcome the baser human impulses; no longer by repression, but by the spread of enlightened altruism.

Much of this is implicit in Naomi Mitchison's book. For instance, commenting on the departure of Aldous Huxley, Auden and others for America on the eve of war, as 'a break that was difficult to heal', she adds: 'No doubt we who stayed felt both pride and resentment; we were living real life, they were out of it. Both are rather nasty emotions.'

One might wish for a more explicit statement of the codes of conduct sought in those inter-war years. She did begin, but all of our efforts were swept away in September 1939.

Naomi Mitchison was one of the most 'liberated' women of her generation: just because she plunged into that thorny thicket of human relations, whether in sex, race or class, undeterred – but also unprotected – by political dogmas or affiliations. It is a pity that, for reasons I indicated, the story of her explorations is at present scrappy and incomplete. None the less, her approach may well prove more relevant, fundamental and fruitful than the political drive for new rules and laws.

Her life accords with her code; a life entirely concerned with creation, whether in mind, spirit, or ordinary practical affairs. To me this represents what (stripped of labels of class or degree of intelligence) is meant by being a woman. We 'may well ask' how far these creative, potentially reconciling powers of women are active, or even recognised – by both sexes – in our quarrelsome, violent society of today.

Alexandra Kollontai: A Biography
by Cathy Porter

If she had not been a woman, the fame of Alexandra
Kollontai might well exceed that of Lenin and other great
revolutionary leaders of her period, or indeed, of all history.
Because she espoused the cause of women and was not an
orthodox bolshevik, she has never been given a place of
honour in her own country. And because she was a revolutionary, she has not received her due from the movement for
women's emancipation.

Today, when it is no longer possible to separate liberating women from all the other much needed social and
economic changes, the breadth and depth of Alexandra
Kollontai's insight will, I hope, be recognised. To this
recognition Cathy Porter's biography, based on such wide-
ranging research and grasp of political issues, can make a
very effective and important contribution. Yet how, in these
moments of more than usually sordid cold war exchanges,
can people be moved to understand all that led up to, and was
meant by, the bolshevik revolution of 1917?

Alexandra Kollontai, who was born in 1872, was herself
the child of an unusual marriage. Her mother, Alexandra
Masalina, daughter of an emancipated Finnish peasant
turned wood merchant, had been married off, apparently
suitably, by her father, though she and a young Russian
cavalry officer were desperately in love. Later, in the face of
the scandal it caused in those times, and despite her three
children by her first husband, Alexandra obtained a divorce

and married the man she loved. Peasant and aristocrat – not to mention faith in true love – were mingled in Alexandra Kollontai's heredity.

The Russian society in which she grew up was still semi-feudal: a veneer of upper class comfort and luxury covered the great mass of the illiterate, poverty-stricken and oppressed. Large family households comprised various demanding elderly relatives, and numerous ill-paid and not too well nourished servants, to wait on them all. In such a well-to-do home a child would be spoiled with every kind of attention and amusement. Though Kollontai's mother was unconventional in that she discarded the crinoline and boned stays, opened the windows to fresh air, read George Sand and Herbert Spencer, she nonetheless treated her daughter like a pampered aristocrat, objected to her associating with the servants and the poor and regarded her marriage to Vladimir Kollontai – a young man qualifying as an engineer and factory inspector – as a *mésalliance* beneath her class.

Alexandra Kollontai's sympathy, however, even in her early years, lay with her peasant playmates; a compassion which she shared with increasing numbers of her generation, especially women. In the ferment of ideas stimulated by economic and industrial development in Europe, Russia's adolescents were demanding education, which to the tsarist government spelt sedition. Consequently numbers of young women students, among them Alexandra Kollontai, trekked to Zurich University, to qualify for medicine and other professions, so that they might go with missionary zeal to help and educate the emancipated serfs. An industrial proletariat as yet scarcely existed, though Kollontai immediately became aware of the miserable conditions of the women workers in the factories she visited with her husband.

WOMAN'S ROLE

The part played by Russian women in sowing the seeds of revolution, while they sought also their own emancipation, is little known or understood: maternal care, as it were, expanding beyond the family and broadening out into a passionate social conscience. The revolution that finally broke out in 1917 had not been built up on an advance to power by highly organised trade unions; on the contrary, it was set afire by a burning ideal, nurtured and cherished over the years, by a handful of men and women intellectuals, many of them bourgeois or aristocratic.

For these potential revolutionaries, work for the cause came before family responsibilities. Domestic cares were too narrow to contain them: before long Comrade Kollontai (as I have always called her) had left husband and son and was among the many subversives under constant threat of police arrest. From that time till the day of her death the primary driving force of Kollontai's life was the great revolutionary ideal. Already, by 1904, Lenin had realised her value; she was to be the only woman in his government in 1917.

The fortunes of the true revolutionary cause through two world wars are brilliantly traced in this book – for that alone it is compulsive reading. More significant and relevant today perhaps is the relation to that revolution of – most especially – this one woman.

Kollontai had a clear bright mind. She could, as the saying was, think like a man. She was never content with half-truth; she disliked half-measures. Though she wrote countless articles, pamphlets and books about the care of mothers and children, and motherhood and society, no one, least of all herself, would have called Kollontai a motherly person. In revolt against the rights of possession of wives and children enjoyed by men, to her as to others of her contemporaries, responsibilities for the care of mothers and children rested on the whole community. This did not mean, as their enemies contended, the cold-hearted takeover of children by the state. In fact, the problem of family versus state is still unsolved in industrial societies today.

Kollontai had lovers who were her comrades in the revolutionary struggle; her entire 'family life' reposed in a remarkable relationship with her son Mikhail (Misha). From the day of his birth in 1893 to his mother's death in 1952, whether they were together or apart, in exile or at home, that link seems never to have been broken. To me there is meaning in this durable relation: there was at least one man who honoured her with a constant loyalty and respect for her achievements.

Kollontai, often alone, faced virtually every problem of a woman seeking her rights, whether as an individual or as a sex: the lover who sees woman only as a sex object; the male (or female) politician to whom feminism is a tiresome bourgeois red herring in the path of socialism – not to mention the thousand and one arguments about women's lack of education, inferior physical strength, or mind, and the rest.

When, in Moscow in 1920, I asked the comrades what was 'in it' for women in the revolution, I received an astonished answer that they 'supposed women would just go on as usual.' Kollontai herself told me that she felt that wartime conditions were being made an excuse for not taking steps to protect children from exploitation, and to give them proper care. Her words to me are confirmed by Cathy Porter's report of how at this very date, isolated as she was in opposition to official policies, Kollontai persisted in her demand that women should receive greater opportunities and responsibility for re-organising the social structure. Yet woman as individual, as voter, worker, sex partner meant more to her than the traditional maternal role.

Oddly enough, women's demand for the vote was split by class in Russia as elsewhere. Middle class women were active; so, independently, were women workers and wives, though they had other more pressing problems as well.

In 1908, when permission had at last been given for the first All Russian Women's Congress in St Petersburg, Kollontai organised untiringly to get a delegation of working women there to state their case. In daily fear of arrest just then she could not risk speaking, but attended at the back of the hall. Unable to bear the condescension and some insults from the smartly dressed women to her worker comrades, Kollontai 'took the floor to argue.' In the uproar created by her appearance she escaped by the back door, seized her passport and some luggage. The next day she was in Germany, embarked on an exile that was to last for eight and a half years.

She joined the German Socialist Party and, based in Berlin, presently made a living by her books and journalism, speaking and organising incessantly. During this period she visited nearly every country in Europe, and even the United States. On one occasion in London she took part in a May Day demonstration with Bernard Shaw. Almost every one of the Russian creators of the bolshevik revolution – all the great names, among them Lenin, Bukharin, Radek, Zinoviev, Kamenev, Chicherin, were exiled in Europe also, whether in Paris, Geneva, Vienna, or Italy. Gorky, in Capri, was able to publish; he produced the first edition of Kollontai's *Social Basis of the Woman Question* in 1909.

With genial and, often, financial help from Karl Liebknecht, the exiles were able to meet from time to time in Berlin. They could not go into action: frustrated, they spoke, wrote and argued interminably; perhaps exhausted themselves in theorising, or took in too heady draughts of German and marxist thought. Though the revolution was international in design, it might well have been different in content, had it continued to originate from its Russian home base.

For Kollontai, as for others, there was a very bad moment in 1914, when to their socialist comrades, overnight, they became enemy aliens. It also seems to me ironical that, whereas even left-wingers in the west had not bothered to find out much about that far-off country under that dreadful Tsar, the makers of the revolution must have known Europe like the back of their hands. This might have served them well in negotiation, but for the tide of hatred and nationalism stirred up by the war.

Kollontai was sneered at by her male colleagues and censured by some women for her love affairs and her advocacy of free love – to me one of the most remarkable contributions of her thought in its period and setting. She saw already that among young men and women of improving education in factory and urban life there would be love affairs that would mean more than mere sexual satisfaction. She knew also, that for both men and women, even on the physical basis, but on equal terms, there could be a far richer love experience than was afforded by the old marital institutions.

The care that the state could give to children would set

free mothers who wanted to work, but it could also set free both parents from a lifelong, close family partnership. Her male colleagues thought of marriage in terms of economics; they were changing society, too, on the basis of economic equality, justice, mechanical order. Her insight went deeper. There is more to life than measuring work, skill and money.

What matters is the code of human relations by which men, women and children in the new society should live. Love need not be suffering; it could be bright and joyful so long as it was not based on money and blood ties. This proviso is important. She thought that love, as a sensitive awareness of personality between two human beings, had an overriding importance in overcoming spiritual isolation and could 'become the cult of humanity.'

In the same year, 1920, as I stood beside Kollontai in the great Women's Congress in the Bolshoi theatre in Moscow, I expressed in an article my misgivings about the machine age; my fears that communists and socialists, stressing economics to the exclusion of less material values, would end up as nothing but capitalists themselves. Perhaps Kollontai and I shared the same misgivings; perhaps the same dreams; I was 26. I have carried with me since then two major convictions: one, that women must have a far larger part in the direction of affairs; two, that the cold war should never have begun and must be ended.

Part Fourteen

OPINION

1982

Requested to take up her pen again for the newspapers, Dora Russell was asked to write her *Opinion* for a Sunday paper. Having submitted her 'opinion' it was rejected and a rewrite called for. She rewrote – and again it was rejected. Her experience confirmed her suspicion that while professing to encompass a range of opinions most editors only publish those which are consistent with their own views of the world. Both versions are included here.

WHY, WHEN WOMEN DO SO MUCH WORK DO THEY HAVE SO LITTLE MONEY OR POWER?

Version 1

Women are 50 per cent of the world's population; put in two thirds of the world's working hours; receive 10 per cent of the world's income and own less that 1 per cent of world property. Nearly half the labour force in India's building industry are women. Girls get little or no education.

Turn from these admittedly disgraceful world statistics to our own 'civilised' society. Englishwomen hoped to attain power on equal terms with men by their war for votes and seats in a democratic Parliament. The results of this agonising struggle are negligible. Deep-seated prejudice obstructs the selection or success of women Parliamentary candidates. Hence a parallel campaign has to be pursued, inch by inch, for women's rights to higher education, entry to the professions, law, medicine, administration, headships of schools and institutions, in fact every position that confers authority or power. Conversely factory and mine owners, and the sweat shops welcomed the opportunity to exploit the cheap labour of mothers with their plentiful supply of child workers. The mothers' assertion – in the 1920s – of their right to limit the numbers of these children is even now still the subject of bitter political controversy.

Commentators tell us that it is up to women themselves now to take advantage of opportunities which they have gained. They point to a woman Prime Minister. They, as well as many women, ignore the fact that to take any part in power politics a woman must play the masculine role and accept the entirely male chauvinist values on which human society had been based for thousands of years.

There is one striking difference. To-day it is said that equality with men involves drafting women into the armed services. In the distant past, though women were the booty of conquerors in wars, there was no demand that women should be soldiers. I believe that that basic structure of our society ought from the beginning to have been shaped by women rather than men, since the concept of the family and concern for the race reside primarily in women. Women are better organisers, better able to see society as many differing groups and types whose needs must be catered for.

England once had a Queen who was an absolute monarch and who refused to take a consort. About her in admiration, her Minister Francis Bacon wrote: 'Elizabeth was a wonderful person among women, a memorable person among princes . . . this same humour of her people over eager for war and impatient of peace, did not prevent her from maintaining peace during the whole time of her reign'. On religion: 'her intention was . . . not to force consciences . . . but not to let the state under pretence of conscience and religion, be brought in danger'.

We might begin to shape a society of at least equal power between men and women by the principle of the 'coupled vote' suggested by Bernard Shaw. In each constituency parties would put up a man and a woman; *both* be voted for. By doubling the size of each constituency there need be no increase in number of M.P.s actually taking their seats. But half the house would be men and half women. Committees, radio and television programmes would also be men and women in equal numbers.

Women have changed. The kind of women I meet to-day did not exist when I was young. They are wide awake to the state of the world brought about by the disastrous follies of male government. Men would be well advised to listen to what in very many countries their women are saying.

Men should stop nonsensical condescension, give women their full rights in power and partnership. And not only listen to women but act on their advice. With such a true Partnership it may still not be too late to end the nuclear and armament idiocy.

Then we could use the creative powers which all of us

possess to make life on this planet not only worth living, but also great fun.

Version 2

When women are 50 per cent of the world's population, put in two thirds of the world's working hours; receive 1.4 per cent of the world's income and own less that 1 per cent of world property, why do they have so little power?

Turn from these admittedly disgraceful world statistics to our own civilised society.

By the British Constitution Parliament is the Sovereign Power. Accordingly, women in Britain demanded the right to vote for its members; and for women, if elected, to take their seats, together with the men. But ingrained prejudice among electors and selection committees has meant that in a House of Commons of over 600 members there sits a mere handful of women.

To redress the balance Bernard Shaw once proposed the 'coupled vote'; a scheme by which, in every constituency, each party should put up two candidates, a man and a woman. Electors must vote for both. Any ballot paper that disregarded this rule would be disqualified. By altering the boundaries of constituencies, making each twice its present size and numbers, Parliament would still consist of some 600 members, but half would be men and half women.

On paper this sounds sensible and feasible. But it could well be simply a way to delude the public into believing that the power to govern was now divided equally between women and men.

Equal is a deceptive word. Many people think equal means identical. Much depends on why women want power. Is it in order to see their ideals and aims prevail, or have more weight in the main purposes of society, or for more money and personal liberty? If women think identically with men, then, apart from ambition for careers, it does not matter if the members of Parliament are men or women.

In my opinion women should combine their assertion of equality with the assertion of their differences. If, in fact, women were in equal numbers with men in Parliament, the very nature of that institution would cause them rapidly to identify with the male image. Parliament is men's substitute for civil war or duelling. Its traditions and procedure are founded on the male structure of society, scoring off the other fellow, or party, in debate, a male belligerence, that has gone on for thousands of years. It is not surprising that advocates of equality for women should also take it for granted that women should play an equal part with men in the armed forces. Yet in all the years of women's subjection it was never suggested that a function of women was to be soldiers, a career which most women would prefer their men not to follow.

To take an active part in the current style of politics, women have to accept the male structure of society and play the masculine role according to the rules of the game. Yet the natural instinct of women in social and governmental organisations is not divisive but for cohesion, consensus and co-operation; to seek a solution, not a victory for one side. They take note of individual needs and try to reconcile them and are more concerned with the fate of our species.

England once had a Queen who was an absolute monarch and who refused to take a consort. About her in admiration her minister Francis Bacon wrote: 'Elizabeth was a wonderful person among women, a memorable person among princes . . . this same humour of her people over-eager for war and impatient of peace did not prevent her from maintaining peace during the whole time of her reign'. On religion, 'her intention was . . . not to force consciences . . . but not to let the state under pretence of conscience and religion, be brought in danger'.

Women have changed. The kind of women I meet to-day did not exist when I was young. As more of them take part in the professions and other work outside the home, they are wide awake to the present disastrous state of the world.

But women have no real power to change things. Because of this, during the whole period, of some seventy-five years, that I have worked in women's movements, I have seen their conferences, resolutions, petitions totally disregarded. Bills which they sponsored in Parliament have been defeated, shockingly delayed, or, once passed, assailed again in the attempt to undo them.

Men would be well advised to listen to what women in very many countries are now saying. The contribution offered by the thought of women is vital. Let a period recognising true equality – not identity – between the sexes begin, especially in the influential countries, then equal representation would have a real value.

True partnership between men and women has never existed in all history. Starting from harmony between the sexes, it would have an amazing result on human affairs throughout the world.

Part Fifteen

CHALLENGE TO HUMANISM

1982

Once more Dora Russell returns to some of the themes of her youth and reveals her remarkable consistency over more than sixty years.

CHALLENGE TO HUMANISM

As *The Freethinker* enters its second century, it and the National Secular Society meet challenges by antagonists who are likely to prove as daunting as the enemies faced by the 19th-century pioneers like Charles Bradlaugh, Annie Besant and G. W. Foote.

The human race is confronted not only by the old struggle for freedom of thought but, under nuclear threat, for sheer physical survival. Humanity is now locked in a grim conflict that is being waged at all levels; in politics, economics, ideologies, religion, philosophy, science, ecology. Yet so departmentalised are our minds and our social structure, that contenders involved in one field are too often unaware that the same struggle, on precisely the same issues, is going on in all the others. Are humanists fully awake to what threatens us all, and how important it may be to give a lead, seek allies and sound the alarm to arouse the sleepers?

In the issue of *The Freethinker* for November 1981, some articles indicate the directions from which the attack is coming. There is the usual entrenched faith of the established Christian churches, observing, in the customary Armistice Day ceremonial, their adherence to the doctrine of just wars. Today there are many sincere Christians, already pacifists, who are joining CND. But despite their creed of brotherly love they would still not subscribe to the sentiments of John Lennon's song: 'Imagine there is no heaven, no separate countries, no religions to die for.'

On the contrary, President Reagan's 'twice born' evangelical Protestants are out to crush the humanists and sweep the country in a vast conversion to faith in America as god's favoured nation, destined to rule the world. For these 'creationists' the scientists' theory of man's evolution is so much nonsense, but science is splendid when devoted to preparations for war.

The non-Christian religions of the Middle East are newly athirst for killing and dying and persecuting; direct opposition to all that America stands for. Then there are the Marxist-Leninist believers with their varying sects in Russia and China.

In Britain, politicians, economists and trade unionists are split on the dilemmas of disarmament; querying whether to spend money on nuclear weapons or welfare, war or peace, death or life. The clash between these two claimants on the national wealth is not new. It has merely reached its present critical stage because of the immense growth of the contending claimants. On the one side the hungry millions of the world (as well as our own now more demanding citizens); on the other, a vast number of ever more diabolical, scientifically ingenious and horribly expensive weapons with which wars may now be waged.

No country or people can now escape that ultimate war, to which persistence in our way of life and belief has brought the pursuit of rivalry, prosperity and power, supported by the expansion of scientific discovery and the resultant industrial technology.

Revolt by the younger generation against science is the natural outcome of the bomb on Hiroshima, followed by the mounting tension of the so-called 'balance of terror'. In addition, the young now realise that the boosted technology, with automation, is rendering human labour redundant; consequently not only they, but even their fathers and mothers, are out of work. In such times people tend to turn to the comforts of religion. And the holders of power are well satisfied that the populace should be distracted from the subversion that might otherwise result from their frustration and discontent.

Some believers return to the neglected churches. The religious teaching in the schools (to which agnostics and atheists justly object) may still indoctrinate, but it no longer has an emotional appeal that inspires the young.

THE FAILURE OF RELIGION

Strenuous efforts are being made on television and radio to reclaim their parents. The BBC is very active. Three pages a week in the *Listener* offer to teach us about the remission of our sins, salvation and the mysteries of theology. Television provides us with the unedifying spectacle of masses of grown men and women bawling about Jesus while prancing and stamping like pop groups.

We are also shown the orgiastic antics (significantly blindfold) of those who follow a new religious practice taught by a guru, which for younger people appears to be a more popular outlet for the emotions and a means of saving your own soul.

It is with these young men and women, above all, that we should be concerned. What do their elders offer them but religions in which they can no longer believe, or faith in that rationalism and science which, in their view, have brought them to the edge of destruction and do not even offer the minimum security of employment?

It is no use talking to young people about the wonders of electronics, or the splendid technology that is going on, to make some people, but probably not them, exceedingly prosperous. What they see is a society in which the best scientific brains – and the most money – are devoted to research and industry for war purposes, and an education increasingly concentrated on the limited amount of manpower that will be needed to serve the scientific elite. They may well ask the one vital question: 'Since the statesmen and scientists are so clever, why do they not put an end to war?'

The young, and to some extent also their parents, are starved of expression of feeling, of creative outlets, colour, adventure, variety, change. With nothing but small subsidies from the State, how are they to fill their days of enforced leisure? Sex (for the most part perforce without parenthood), and the new style religions are all that they have left. Some, in desperation, take to violence in the streets; some take their own lives.

Fanny Cockerell, of the Progressive League, in her article ('A Dormitory of Bishops,' November 1981), touches on this problem of the need to have something to believe in and for the comfort of fellowship with other human beings. As one who supported the foundation of the League, who were welcomed for their conferences at my school, I am glad to know that *Plan* still lives and the League is still active. They, among those of us who are humanists, know well enough that we had to fight for our causes; free speech, birth control, divorce and abortion law reform – against brutal opposition from organised religion. We know too of the great benefits brought by science, however much overshadowed by the prostitution of science to war. We have consistently cam- paigned against armaments, and longed to see science in alliance with peace. All that we strove for is now clearly under attack by the organised religious hierarchies who will use every device of propaganda and repression to reimpose their authority, attributing all the world's evils to man's sinfulness and disobedience to god.

IGNORING REALITY

The new religions – while perhaps some avoid postulating god, and discard sin – offer instead an almost sexual adoration of their human leader. They retreat into personal isolation, expressed in the quietism of meditation, or else in the deliberate discarding of all inhibitions and the fulfilment of the personality with a degree of self-indulgence which resembles – is perhaps attributable to – the intensely selfish individualism that is characteristic of the Western so-called free world. In that free world, even now, moves against democracy endeavour to repress and outlaw strikes, whilst in that so-called unfree world, the democratic right to strike is being asserted and defended.

With such social issues, with poverty, with the threat of nuclear war, the followers of the new religions are not at all concerned. Their argument that the self must be fulfilled before feeling or showing concern for others is no more than pretence. In actual fact, relatives and friends soon find that absorption in the new religions is destructive of all other sympathy and ties.

What seems to me important is that we are, after all,

social animals, and it is only by knowing and helping and being helped by others, that we ourselves realise what, in modern jargon, is called our potential. Religious communities, like convents and monasteries, have always existed for those who prefer to retire from the tumult of the secular world. But the soul-seekers of today should realise that the nuclear world is not like that of the dying Roman Empire. If, by chance, some survive the nuclear holocaust, on a tiny islet, the destroyed and poisoned land will be unproductive and uninhabitable. There is no escape.

God alone, the religious might say, can and will resolve the intolerable confusion which human beings have brought upon themselves. We might reply that the very notion of a god was evoked by men and women in order to evade their own responsibilities. It is time for humanity to reach maturity and at long last assume responsibility – as far as it in us lies – for creating a tolerable existence for everything that lives on our planet.

HUMANITY'S OPPORTUNITIES

In humanism I have always felt the warmth of association with all organic life, with our roots in the productive soil of our earth. My dissent from god and religion arose from its denial of this very life which animates plants, birds, animals and humans. If god created all this, then why are his worshippers commanded to reject it all, as savage, bestial, lust and sin?

Human beings have developed remarkable gifts of imagination and rational thought. These come from the living organisms that are ourselves and the energy that moves us, as it moves everything else, to grow, create, reach old age and die. With all our faculties we shape our image of the external world. Imagination serves our dreams and aspirations; it may also serve our fears, reason, our curiosity as to what is really real, which may also act as a bridle on our imagination. If we, and our statesmen, were to apply to international politics the long-suffering patience, imagination and honesty of purpose of the artist or scientist in their work, we could save our world from disaster and bring about some tolerance, harmony and peace. At this time this is more important than detailed argument about our origins, or from where the force of creative life comes.

It seems to me as if, at present, fear is driving many to evade the issue. Radio and television provide another escape. The people seen and heard on the interminable television serials have become more real to those who watch them than their fellow citizens, or fellow travellers on this planet. We live in a real world, which is in great danger from our ignorance and foolish mistakes.

Humanism should be active. It has much to contribute. Above all it is not a new religion with doctrines, merely the plea that customs and beliefs are personal and never justify persecution or indifference to others. If we examine ourselves and reflect on what power-seeking, killing and fear have done to a world of plenty and great beauty and its peoples, we may learn how it is possible to live as human beings, and take courage to do so.

SOURCES

Hypatia was first published in the To-day and To-morrow series by Kegan Paul, Trench, Trubner, London, in 1925.

The Right To Be Happy was first published by George Routledge & Sons, London, in 1927.

In Defence of Children was first published by Hamish Hamilton, London, in 1932.

The *El Sol* articles were first published in that journal between 1926 and 1930.

'Your Baby: All He Will Need in His First Year' was first published in the *Sunday Chronicle*, 19 February 1933.

'We Called On Europe' was written in 1959 and is published here for the first time.

'In a Man's World: The Eclipse of Woman' was first published in *Anarchy* 56 (Vol. 5, No. 10), October 1965.

'Thinking about Time' was first published in the *Cornish Review* in 1969.

'The Biological Strength of Women' was first published in *Women Speaking* in 1973.

'The Long Campaign' was first published in the *New Humanist*, December 1974, and is reprinted by permission of the Rationalist Press Association.

'Threats to Freedom' was first published in the *New Humanist* in 1978 and is reprinted by permission of the Rationalist Press Association.

The review of Naomi Mitchison's *All Change Here* was first published in the *New Humanist*, August 1975, and is reprinted by permission of the Rationalist Press Association.

The review of Naomi Mitchison's *You May Well Ask* was first published in the *New Humanist*, Autumn 1979, and is reprinted by permission of the Rationalist Press Association.

The review of *Alexandra Kollontai: A Biography* was first published in *New Society*, 28 February 1980.

'Challenge to Humanism' was first published in *The Freethinker*, Vol. 102, No. 1, January 1982.

INDEX